Fathers as Primary Caregivers

**Recent Titles in
Contributions in Family Studies**

Women in the Family and the Economy: An International Comparative Survey
George Kurian and Ratna Ghosh, editors

Revolutions in Americans' Lives: A Demographic Perspective on the History of
Americans, Their Families, and Their Society
Robert V. Wells

Three Different Worlds: Women, Men, and Children in an Industrializing Community
Frances Abrahamer Rothstein

Family and Work: Comparative Convergences
Merlin B. Brinkerhoff, editor

Child-Rearing and Reform: A Study of the Nobility in Eighteenth-Century Poland
Bogna Lorence-Kot

Parent-Child Interaction in Transition
George Kurian, editor

The Dutch Gentry, 1500–1650: Family, Faith, and Fortune
Sherrin Marshall

Migrants in Europe: The Role of Family, Labor, and Politics
Hans Christian Buechler and Judith-Maria Buechler, editors

A History of Marriage Systems
G. Robina Quale

Feeding Infants in Four Societies: Causes and Consequences of Mothers' Choices
Beverly Winikoff, Mary Ann Castle, Virginia Hight Laukaran, editors

The Reconstruction of Family Policy
Elaine A. Anderson and Richard C. Hula, editors

Family, Justice, and Delinquency
Brenda Geiger and Michael Fischer

Fathers as Primary Caregivers

BRENDA GEIGER

Foreword by Joan Newman

Contributions in Family Studies, Number 17

Greenwood Press
Westport, Connecticut • London

Library of Congress Cataloging-in-Publication Data

Geiger, Brenda.
    Fathers as primary caregivers / Brenda Geiger ; foreword by Joan
Newman.
        p.   cm.—(Contributions in family studies, ISSN 0147–1023;
    no. 17)
    Includes bibliographical references and index.
    ISBN 0–313–29919–6 (alk. paper)
    1. Father and infant.   2. Mother and infant.   3. Parent and
infant.   4. Attachment behavior.   5. Child care—psychological aspects.
6. Sex role.   I. Title.   II. Series.
    BF720.F38G45   1996
    155.6′462—dc20   95–41688

British Library Cataloguing in Publication Data is available.

Library of Congress Catalog Card Number: 95–41688
ISBN: 0–313–29919–6
ISSN: 0147–1023

First published in 1996

Greenwood Press, 88 Post Road West, Westport, CT 06881
An imprint of Greenwood Publishing Group, Inc.

Printed in the United States of America

To Our Beloved Children

Adina, Danielle, Arielle, Avital, and Eliana

and Their Dedicated Father

Who Made This Work Possible

Contents

Tables

Foreword by Joan Newman

This book is about change in long-standing traditions and the creative maintenance of security and stability in the midst of that change. Reconfigured nuclear families, economic uncertainties, and redefinitions in gender roles are all resulting in the movement of mothers into the work force. The traditional institution of the family is faltering as men and women set new goals for their survival and for their fulfillment. These changes create a new and uncertain context for child rearing.

Through extensive videotaping of twenty-eight infants and their parents interacting in their own homes, as well as probing interviews with the parents, Brenda Geiger shows the variety of ways in which child care and careers are being combined and negotiated in middle-class America today. In half of the families studied, fathers have become their infant's primary caregiver. In the remaining families, mothers have retained that role but not without acknowledging pressures to do otherwise. Generously sharing their experiences with the researcher, all of the parents recognize their responsibility to provide their infants with stability and quality care. Geiger's exciting finding is that fathers and mothers are able to do it equally well. Fathers who are their infant's primary caregiver are able to provide their child with emotional security and sensitive care. With minor differences in style, especially play style, these fathers are able to comfort, amuse, and attend to all physical needs of their infants in the manner traditionally considered "natural" to mothers. Geiger's well-controlled and insightful procedures allow these parents to show that gender does not determine parenting sensitivity and capability.

Drawing especially from the research, writing, and methodology of attachment theorists, Geiger provides a concise explication of the major theories of child development to explain the significance of the new role for fathers. However, the most powerful justification for studying the fathers' new role is practical. Mothers are in the work force, infants need care, and the community provision of such care is perceived to be inadequate. Time and again in the interviews, parents express uncertainty about using day care, which they feel is insufficiently responsive to each child's needs. Their lack of security is shared by child development experts who counsel reexamination of the effects of day care and of circumstances in which it can be a satisfactory environment for young children's development.

Thus, this book is about finding security in the stress that modern society thrusts upon families. Most of the families described have constructed routines and relationships adapted to their own circumstances and protective of the essential bonding between infant and caregiver. Geiger's important work describes the small gestures and intimate responses from which primary caregivers, fathers as well as mothers, construct their relationships. Although not all primary caregiving fathers realized the central role they played, their involvement in child care "unleashed fathers' undiscovered potential as competent and nurturant caregivers" (Geiger).

And as the data make abundantly clear, by their ability to establish a secure base in which their infants can develop independence, primary caregiving fathers also provide a secure base for their spouse. Mothers in the study were freed to leave households, seek employment options, and return home secure in the knowledge that there was shared emotional fulfillment in the household. As one secondary caregiving mother expressed it, "People tell me that it is easy for me, because I know that [my husband] is staying at home with [the baby]. They tell me that if he was in day care I would not feel as comfortable." Current United States census data show that in 1991 father care of infants under one year of age with mothers in the work force constituted 21.6 percent of all child-care arrangements (*Statistical Abstract of the United States 1994*, No. 114, p. 386). We are fortunate to have Geiger's book to document the outcomes of this increasingly common arrangement.

The message of this book is hopeful. Despite reports of disintegrating nuclear families, of "deadbeat" fathers, of loss of community traditions and supports, and of drastic changes in gender roles, the essential child-rearing function of families can persist. In those families where fathers remain at home to care for their infant, family roles have changed, but their functions are honored. The various patterns of reciprocal roles revealed by the traditional and less-traditional parents show that society can harness a variety of models for ensuring the healthy development of the next generation.

Having lived in several countries (France, Egypt, Israel, Germany, Italy, and the United States), Geiger is aware of the diversity, potential and problems of different child-rearing practices. Her lively and penetrating mind, boundless energy and motivation, determination to complete her third book, and five young children, inevitably challenged Geiger to investigate creative ways of combining responsible parenting with a personal role broadened from housework and child care. Given that the five children are daughters, she is especially motivated to study and model equitable alternatives to the comfortable yet confining maternal role. As Geiger writes, "Egalitarian child rearing does not begin by giving dolls to boys and trucks to girls, but by modeling." Geiger herself gave her older girls both a research model and a camcorder; they cooperated in the crucial role of filming the participants' interactions, while the younger children remained at home in the care of their father. The completion of this book is itself a testimony to the achievement resulting from role change and flexibility.

Joan Newman
State University of New York at Albany

Acknowledgments

I would like to especially thank Dr. Joan Newman for sharing with me her expertise and thoughts on child development and Dr. Reuben Rusch for sharing with me his knowledge in research design. I would also like to express my appreciation to William Schwarz and Dr. Michael Green for their assistance in computer science and SPSS. Thanks to Dr. Michael Fischer for his help in producing tables and for his editorial comments. Finally, my grateful thanks to my two daughters, Adina and Danielle, for videotaping the last episode of the observation, and to the parents and infants for sharing with me precious time in the privacy of their homes.

Introduction

It is 8 A.M. Mr. Baker is rocking his baby John while standing at the window and waving to his spouse leaving the driveway to work at the state campus. Since John's birth, Mr. Baker has taken advantage of his flexible working hours to take care of their son during the day. He changes his diapers, feeds him, kisses and hugs him, and sings lullabies to put him to sleep. Mr. Smith, their neighbor, leaves for work at the same time as Mrs. Baker. He honks his horn to say good-bye to his spouse and baby daughter, Julie. Mr. Smith is also a state employee. He does not spend any time with Julie during the day. He does not change her diapers or put her to sleep. Maybe, if he does not have a late meeting this evening, he will play with her and give her a bath. Mrs. Smith has temporarily abandoned her career to take care of Julie full-time.

Is Mr. Baker as competent and skillful as Mrs. Smith in assuming primary caregiving duties? Is he as nurturant and affectionate as Mrs. Baker is? Are there significant differences in their level of skill and affection because men do not beget or nurse children and are not equipped by nature to provide for their infants' needs? Does Mr. Baker's son John exhibit the same affiliative and attachment behaviors toward his father as Julie does toward her mother, or do their behaviors significantly differ despite the fact that Mr. Baker and Mrs. Smith are both primary caregivers?

Within the past twenty-five years many sociological and ideological changes have resulted in fathers' greater involvement in child care. These include changes in sex-role definitions, changes in the workplace concerning women's work status, shorter and more-flexible work hours, split jobs in which males and females may share the same position, changes in medical practices and maternity ward visiting arrangements, and fathers' increased participation in prepartum and postpartum childbirth activities (Pedersen,

1980).   Also, with structural unemployment, underemployment, the reduction of working hours and/or workers' load and flexibility in working hours, many men have come to reevaluate the values that were important to them—professional achievement and success versus fatherhood and family life.

Simultaneously, women's greater level of education and qualifications have increased their status and decision power in the workplace and at home. Women no longer feel excluded from the domain that used to be exclusively that of men—professional work—and no longer feel confined to the domain that used to be uniquely assigned to women—child care. Many request that obligations and duties be shared equitably inside and outside the home. An increased number of women with very young children are participating in the work force outside the home. From 1975 to 1993 the rate of employed mothers in intact families with infants less than one year of age increased by 87 percent, namely, from 30.8 to 57.5 percent (*Statistical Abstract of the United States 1994*, No. 114, p. 402). These changes, combined with the growing awareness of the important role fathers play in the socioemotional development of their infants, the potential risks of day care on such development (Belsky, 1988; Sroufe, 1988), as well as the lack of affordable quality day care for infants less than one-year old have led an increasing number of fathers to become their infant's primary caregivers while their spouse is employed full-time outside the home (Defrain, 1979; Field, 1978; Frodi et al., 1983; Gronseth, 1975; Radin, 1980; Russel, 1983; Russel & Radojevic, 1992). In fact, in 1991, father care in the child's home has become the most common child-care arrangement adopted by employed mothers for infants under one year of age (*Statistical Abstract of the United States 1994*, No. 114, p. 386).   However, fathers' competence and performance as primary caregivers and their ability to become primary attachment figures could only be speculated upon given the scarcity of research findings on this topic.

Fathers as Primary Caregivers

1
Theoretical Background on Father-Infant Attachment

PSYCHOANALYTICALLY ORIENTED THEORIES

The role of the father in infancy has been conceptualized in several theories of child development. The implications for fathers assuming a primary caregiving role in child care may be found in the psychoanalytically oriented theories of Freud and Erikson as well as in learning theory, separation-individuation theory, and attachment theory. The two last theories constitute the main theoretical framework of this current study.

The Role of the Father in Freud's Theory

In Freud's theory (1948), the mother-infant bonding "through sucking for nourishment" is at the basis of sexuality and personality development. This relationship is deemed "unique without parallel, established unalterably as the prototype of all later love relations" (Freud, 1948). Nevertheless, Freud (1955) has also acknowledged the emotional tie that infants form with their father at the pre-oedipal stage. The feeling of love and admiration that children have for their father at this period becomes the basis of identification and reality testing. Boys' sexual wishes toward their mother and hostility for their father at the oedipal stage cannot dissolve this love (Machtlinger, 1981). In an analysis of *A Phobia of a Five-Year Old Boy*, Freud (1955) commented about little Hans who was wrestling with the love and hate he was feeling for his father, "This same father whom he could not help hating as a rival, was the same father whom he had always loved and was bound to go on loving, who had been his model, who had been his first playmate, and who had looked after him from his earliest infancy: and this it was that gave rise to the first conflict" (p. 134).

The Role of the Father in Erikson's Theory

Erikson (1950) has broadened Freud's theoretical emphasis to include social as well as sexual influences upon development. Trust versus mistrust and autonomy versus shame and doubt are psychosocial crises infants face in the first two years of life. Healthy resolution of these conflicts depends on the proper balance of the two antithetical elements of each stage. Thus, in the first year of life, the balance between trust and mistrust is a prerequisite for the development of identity and intimacy in adolescence.

Although Erikson (1950) did not specify the extent of fathers' contribution to the development of basic trust and autonomy, there appears to be no biological reason why fathers could not play a significant role in this development. Actually, by mentioning "the parental faith" rather than the maternal faith "which supports the trust emerging in the newborn," Erikson (1950, p. 250) has implicitly included paternal faith in this concept. It may then be assumed that the development of trust is related to a sense of total security that not only mothers but also fathers could provide to their infants by promptly responding to their cues. By contrast, mistrust and later alienation are consequences of parental insensitivity to their infants' signals.

Learning Theory

Some learning theorists (Dollard & Miller, 1950) have echoed Freud's position in behavioral terms. According to these theorists, the primacy of the mother-infant affective bond is the result of the continued association of the mother with the positive sensation of hunger gratification. The drive reduction hypothesis (Hull, 1943) has been challenged and refuted by Harlow's (1961) and by Harlow and Zimmerman's (1959) experiments on Rhesus monkeys. These monkeys were found to cling and prefer the contact of a soft terry cloth mother surrogate to that of a cold wire mother surrogate, even though the latter fed them. Within this perspective fathers as caregivers could be associated with warmth and nurturance, without having to nurse their infants (Lamb, 1981). No need to add that fathers could also always give a bottle to satisfy their infant's hunger drive!

Fathers within the Separation-Individuation Framework

Within the separation-individuation framework (Abelin, 1971, 1975; Forrest, 1967; Leonard, 1966; Mahler, Pine & Bergman, 1975; Winnicott, 1956), fathers' role is to pull their children out of the symbiotic fusion with their mother and thereby allow for their psychological birth and autonomy.

Infants spend the first two months of their lives half-asleep, half-awake, in a state of autism, totally unaware that someone else is satisfying their needs. At two months of age this awareness emerges. Infants then move to a state of *"omnipotent symbiotic dual unity"* with their mother characterized by a total fusion and lack of differentiation between the I and not-I (Mahler, Pine & Bergman, 1975, p. 46). Infants then progress through a process of separation and individuation to achieve autonomy in ego functioning. In the first phase of this process, differentiation, infants seem to have hatched. They become alert and goal directed.

Hatching and differentiation are helped by mothers' availability and predictability of responding, which enable infants to accumulate a "sufficient reservoir of basic trust" in order "to reach out confidently into the 'other-than-mother' world" (Mahler, Pine & Bergman, 1975, p. 59). At this stage, the function of fathers is to provide mothers with the social and emotional support they need to carry out their "primary maternal preoccupation" (Winnicott, 1956). Fathers who fail to fulfill this role may prevent the establishment of a healthy symbiosis and jeopardize their infants' mental health (Henderson, 1982; Winnicott, 1956).

The direct influence of fathers emerges during the two subsequent phases of the separation-individuation process—practicing and rapprochement. The practicing phase begins when infants begin to crawl, that is, around nine months of age, and terminates when infants begin to walk, that is, around fourteen months of age. Infants' locomoting capacities enable them to widen the boundaries of the world they can explore. Mothers are used as a secure base "for refueling through physical contact" (Mahler, Pine & Bergman, 1975, p. 69). At this stage, fathers stimulate their infants' increasing level of skill. Also, by having "other-than-mother" quality, fathers are experienced as new and exciting partners.

At the rapprochement phase, which occurs between fifteen and twenty-four months of age, mothers are rediscovered as separate individuals. Toddlers realize how separate and vulnerable they are and may long to be one with their mother. Simultaneously, they may also fear to be reengulfed by her. Fathers' availability is crucial for individuation. Coming from outside the symbiotic fusion, fathers represent a stabilizing force that offers toddlers a relationship uncontaminated by ambivalence. They provide support and "a breath of fresh air" whenever toddlers are terrified by the idea of being reengulfed into symbiosis (Mahler, Pine & Bergman, 1975). Fathers assist in the separation-individuation process through play interaction. Furthermore, fathers act as socializers by teaching their children to get along with friends and strangers (MacDonald & Parke, 1984; Parsons

& Bales, 1955). As third parties outside this fusion, they are the first model of friendly interaction with the social world. Fathers are thus "the first stranger, the first representative of the outside world" (Forrest, 1967, p. 280). Fathers who fail to provide such an experience because of low involvement in child care lead their children to perceive other people as strangers producing tension and anxiety (Abelin, 1971, 1975, 1980; Forrest, 1967; Mahler, Pine & Bergman, 1975).

ATTACHMENT THEORY

Bowlby (1969) has also criticized Freud's characterization of the mother-infant bond as resulting from hunger gratification. For Bowlby, infants are attached to their mother not merely because she feeds them but because they are born with a biological propensity for attachment. Infants seek and maintain proximity of their caregivers to satisfy their physical needs, to use them as a safe base from which they can explore their environment, and as a source of comfort when they are under stress (Ainsworth, 1967, 1973; Bowlby, 1969).

Nevertheless, infants are not genuinely attached to anyone until they reach six to eight months of age. Newborn to six-month old infants can differentiate between faces on the basis of visual cues and may smile at their mother, father, or any other caregiver, but they neither show clear preference for any one of their caregivers nor protest separation from them (Ainsworth, 1962; Bowlby, 1973). Cognitive developmental theorists such as Piaget (1954) have explained such behavior by the lack of object permanence. In the perceived world of very young infants, people and objects cease to exist and lose their identity whenever they are no longer perceived. They come in and out of existence depending on whether they are perceived or not. Between six to eight months of age infants begin to realize that the existence of people and objects does not depend on its being perceived, and that people and objects continue to exist whether or not they are perceived. Only then does a real attachment relationship appear (Ainsworth et al., 1978; Bell, 1970; Piaget, 1954).

The Attachment and Affiliative Behavioral Systems

To explain genuine attachment, Bowlby (1969) posited an attachment behavioral system distinct from the affiliative behavioral system. This attachment system includes all the behaviors infants exhibit to approach or stay in proximity of their attachment figures, as well as those behaviors that encourage attachment figures to approach or remain in proximity of their infant. The list of behaviors on the basis of which attachment could be inferred includes proximity maintaining, approaching through locomotion, seeking physical contact, clinging, displaying affection, and exploring from a secure base (Ainsworth, 1964). This list is obviously relevant only for locomoting infants because infants who cannot crawl or walk could not exhibit the majority of these behaviors.

The affiliative behavioral system includes behaviors such as looking, smiling, laughing, vocalizing, playing with the adult, and initiating an activity. These behaviors may be exhibited in friendly interactions with fathers, mothers, or any other individual with whom infants are not necessarily attached (Ainsworth, Bell & Stayton, 1974; Lamb, 1977).

Attachment theorists also argue that whereas the affiliative behavioral system is activated under nonstressful conditions, the attachment behavioral system can only be activated under stress. Under the stress produced by a strange situation, an unfamiliar object such as Big Bird or a clown, or an ambiguous stimulus, infants show a marked preference for their mother over their father or any other individual (Bowlby, 1969).

Thus, for many attachment theorists, the primacy of the infant-mother attachment relationship posited by Freud (1948) has remained unchallenged. It is assumed to constitute a permanent internal model that shapes all future emotional relationships and the capacity to feel positively about oneself and others (Belsky, 1986; Bowlby, 1980). Within this model, the father-infant bond could only replicate that of the mother with her infant (Clarke-Stewart, 1980).

Attachment to Fathers

Nevertheless, by shifting the emphasis from physical care to the quality of the attachment between infants and their caregivers, attachment theorists suggested that infants could form strong attachments to persons assuming very few caregiving duties, such as fathers (Ainsworth, 1963; Schaffer & Emerson, 1964). Several studies have shown that newborns could elicit different responses (Applegate, 1987; Emde, 1981) and form different expectations depending on whether they were interacting with their mother or their father. They were more alert and playful and greeted more often their father than their mother upon reunion (Parke & Sawin, 1976, Parke & Tinsley, 1981; Pedersen, 1980; Pedersen & Robson, 1969; Yogman, 1977).

Infants' behavior toward their father in the Strange Situation[1] has also indicated that infants' attachment to their father was qualitatively different from their attachment to their mother and could not be determined on its basis (Bridges, Connell & Belsky, 1988; Grossman & Grossman, 1980; Lamb, 1978c; Main & Weston, 1981).

In light of such data, there was limited empirical support for the assumptions that infants are monotropically attached to their mother (Bowlby, 1969) and that the mother-infant relationship is the prototype for all future attachment relationships (Bowlby, 1969; Freud, 1948). Attachment theory has been revised to incorporate these findings.

Attachment theorists now suggest that infants are biologically predisposed to emit signals such as tracking visually, crying, smiling, vocalizing, clinging, etc., to elicit nurturance and proximity not only to their mother but also to their father or any other caregiver (Ainsworth, Bell & Stayton, 1974; Lamb, 1978b). Consistent and prompt responding to infants' signals leads to infants' perception of adults as concerned, predictable, and reliable and to the formation of secure attachment. By contrast, unpredictable and inconsistent responding yields insecure attachment. Mothers, fathers, and other caregivers, by their different styles of responding, create a different set of expectations and an array of attachment relationships of various qualities and flavors (Bretherton, 1985; Bridges, Connell & Belsky, 1988; Sroufe, 1988).

STATEMENT OF THE PROBLEM AND RESEARCH PURPOSE

Over the past twenty-five years, fathers' involvement in parenthood has increased (Parke & O'Leary, 1976; Pedersen et al., 1979; Russel, 1983). Fathers been found able to assume caregiving duties with competence and sensitivity to their newborns' needs (Lamb, 1976a, Parke & O'Leary, 1976; Parke & Sawin, 1975; Yogman et al., 1976). They were as competent as mothers in holding, feeding, cuddling, and talking motherese to their infants (Gleason, 1975; Greenberg & Morris, 1974; Kauffman, 1977; Parke & O'Leary, 1976; Parke & Tinsley, 1981). However, fathers' accessibility to their infants remained limited during the first year of life.

Cross-cultural comparisons based on the self-report of traditional parents indicated that fathers in the United States were spending between 1.7 hours (Pleck & Rustad, 1980) to 2.8 hours per week (Kotelchuck, 1976) interacting with their infant. This figure compares to the 1.6 hours per week that European fathers spent with their infant (Newland, 1980). In Kotelchuck's study (1976), 43 percent of U.S. fathers, and in Russel's study (1983), 50 percent of Australian fathers, reported that they had never changed a diaper. A more recent survey conducted in Israel (Ninio & Rinott, 1988), indicated that secondary caregiving fathers continued to be of restricted availability to their infant (2.75 hours per week), and on average performed one caregiving activity per day!

During that limited time spent with their infant, fathers have been found to center their interaction around play. Their role was affiliative. By contrast, mothers' role revolved around caregiving and nurturance (Bailey, 1982; Bretherton, 1985; Lamb & Goldberg, 1982; MacDonald & Parke, 1984; Parsons & Bales, 1955). The exception to this typical pattern of interaction occurs with fathers who have become their infant's primary caregivers and thus combine caregiving and affection with affiliative duties. The question is whether primary caregiving fathers are as capable as mothers of performing caregiving and nurturant duties and of becoming primary attachment figures for their infants. If so, does this influence the extent to which they will retain or lose their role as play partners and primary affiliative figures? The purpose of this study is to sort out the unique and interactive effects of the gender of the caregiver and the primacy of the caregiving role upon the affiliative and attachment behaviors of the caregivers toward their infants and upon the behaviors of the infants toward their caregivers.

NOTE

1. The Strange Situation is the most commonly used method to study the security of the attachment of infants twenty months of age and younger (Ainsworth et al., 1978; Ainsworth & Wittig, 1969). This laboratory procedure consists of eight episodes of increasing stress in which infants are separated and then reunited to their mother in the presence or absence of a stranger.

2

Literature Review on Father-Infant Interaction

TRADITIONAL FATHER-INFANT INTERACTION

A review of the literature comparing the interaction of traditional fathers and traditional mothers with their infant has shown the nature and style of their interaction to be qualitatively different. Mothers' interaction with their infant has been associated with nurturance and affection; that of fathers with affiliation and play (Belsky, 1979; Clarke-Stewart, 1980; Lamb, 1976a; Parke & O' Leary, 1976; Parke & Sawin, 1980; Pedersen, 1980).

Fathers' play interaction with their infant has been found to be totally different from the docile and verbal interaction of mothers with their infant. Whether observed playing with two-week to thirty-month old infants in a laboratory playroom (Yogman, 1977; Yogman et al., 1976) or in their natural home environment, fathers engaged in play involving physical contact with their children. They provided staccato bursts of physical and social stimulation (Yogman et al., 1976), vigorous tactile stimulation (Clarke-Stewart, 1978, 1980; Lamb, 1976a, 1977, 1981), physical tapping, limb moving (Yogman et al., 1976), lifting infants in the air, putting them upside down, or bouncing them up and down (Lamb, 1976b, 1977; Lytton, 1976; Parke & Tinsley, 1981; Weinraub, & Frankel, 1977). This play style was often idiosyncratic, unpredictable, and unusual (Belsky, 1980; Golinkoff & Ames, 1977; Lamb, 1976a, 1977, 1981; Pedersen, 1980; Weinraub & Frankel, 1977).

Fathers' rough-and-tumble play style has also been found to be very exciting and pleasurable to infants. Fathers' play bids were positively answered and their play interaction generally preferred to that of mothers (Clarke-Stewart, 1980; Lamb, 1981). With few exceptions (Ban & Lewis, 1974; Feldman & Ingham, 1975), most studies on infants less than twenty months of age have indicated that by all measures of infants' affiliative behavior—looking, smiling, vocalizing, laughing, and greeting—fathers were preferred to mothers (Clarke-Stewart, 1980; Keller et al., 1975). Aside from the anticipation of an exciting play interaction, this preference has also been attributed to the novelty effect fathers produce on their infants when they reappear after the many hours spent at work away from home (Belsky, 1980; Clarke-Stewart, 1978; Lamb, 1976a, 1981).

Infants' preferential attachment toward each one of their parents has also been researched and found to depend on whether the situation in which infants were observed was stress-free or stressful. In stress-free situations, longitudinal home observations with infants seven to thirteen months of age indicated similar attachment behaviors toward either one of the parents. Infants sought proximity, approached, touched, cried, or protested separation from their father as much as they did that from their mother (Kotelchuck, 1976; Lamb, 1976a, 1978c, 1981).

Attachment theorists objected to these findings by arguing that only under stress could the attachment behavioral system become activated and true preferential attachment emerge. When in need of protection and comfort, infants focus on primary attachment figures and reduce interaction with secondary attachment figures. Thus, only under stress could a hierarchy in attachment relationships appear (Bowlby, 1969). Several procedures have been used to verify this hypothesis including separation protest, proximity seeking, social referencing in the presence of an unfamiliar object or an ambiguous stimulus, and the Strange Situation.

By the criteria of separation protest, nine-month old infants have been found under stress to protest and react with the same degree of distress to separation from father or mother (Kotelchuck et al., 1975; Lamb, 1976a). Unexpectedly, however, the intensity with which infants protested separation from their parents was found to be inversely related to the degree of fathers' involvement in child care. Infants of highly involved fathers cried and disrupted their play least, whereas infants who had low interacting fathers protested separation most (Kotelchuck, 1972; Spelke et al., 1973).

These findings could be explained within the framework of the separation-individuation model. Fathers who are highly involved in child care allow their infants to reach a high level of separation and individuation and to become autonomous. A second interpretation is that fathers' high involvement in child care enables infants to more easily extinguish the anxiety associated with their mother's departure (Spelke, et al., 1973). The negative correlation between fathers' degree of involvement and separation protest has weakened the validity of separation protest as a reliable indicator of attachment for home-reared infants (Lamb, 1979).

Secure-base behavior is another index of attachment. Primary attachment figures are used as a safe base from which infants can explore a strange environment. Comparison of the extent of exploration, as measured by eye contact with a stranger while in proximity of fathers, mothers, or when alone, has indicated that eye contact with a stranger was most intense while in mothers' proximity, less intense while in fathers' proximity, and least intense when no one was present (Cohen & Campos, 1974). Thus, based on this criterion, infants are more attached to their mother who provides a safer base for exploration than their father.

The frequency of approach and the time spent in proximity of a parent seemed to be more-sensitive measures of attachment for locomoting infants than exploration from secure base (Cohen & Campos, 1974; Harlow & Zimmerman, 1959; Lewis, Feiring & Weinraub, 1981). Once under stress, ten-month old infants were found to seek proximity and to move faster toward their mother than toward their father in order to use her as a secure base (Cohen & Campos, 1974).

Social referencing, which refers to the tendency to look at significant others in order to clarify an ambiguous situation, was another criteria of infants' preferential attachment (Cohen & Campos, 1974). When in the presence of an ambiguous stimulus, infants have been found to respond to both of their parents' posed facial expressions (Dickstein & Parke, 1988; Hirshberg, 1990; Hirshberg & Svejda, 1990). They became puzzled and distressed whenever their parents produced conflicting signals about an ambiguous stimulus, such as fathers posing a happy face and mothers a fearful one. And although they sought proximity of their mother for comfort, infants continued to respond to both of their parents' signals and to experience tension. Such a tension was at times manifested by avoidant behavior, motor inhibition, sucking, rocking, and affective flatness (Hirshberg, 1990).

The most commonly used procedure to examine the quality of infants' attachment is the Strange Situation. Factor analysis of infants' behavior toward each one of their parents in the Strange Situation indicated increased differentiation between parents with increased levels of stress (Bridges, Connell & Belsky, 1988). Under a low level of stress, as in episode five of the Strange Situation, infants' reactions upon reunion with their mother and father have been found to vary along the same dimensions: (1) proximity and contact seeking versus avoidance, and (2) resistance/ambivalence versus distance. The first dimension differentiated between infants who showed positive proximity-seeking and contact-maintaining behaviors toward either one of their parents and those who avoided them. The second dimension characterized infants who engaged in resistant ambivalent behavior toward either one of their parents as opposed to those who engaged in positive interaction with them, but only from a distance.

When the level of stress increased, as in episode eight of the Strange Situation, infants' behavior upon reunion with their mother continued to vary along the same dimension as in episode five. By contrast, infants' reunion behavior toward their father had changed and became increasingly similar to that exhibited toward strangers. It varied along a new dimension—comfort seeking/unsociability. Comfort seeking differentiated between those infants who engaged in clinging to their father and those who engaged in positive interaction with them, but only from a distance. Unsociability characterized infants who avoided or resisted interaction with their father or with a stranger as opposed to those who sought positive interaction with them.

Infants' preferential attachment under stress has also been found to depend on whether infants could choose between their parents or not. When they did not have any choice, that is, when in the presence of only one of the parents, infants were found to exhibit the same attachment behaviors toward whichever parent was present (Feldman & Ingham, 1975; Lamb, 1976a). When they did have a choice, that is, when both of their parents were present, a hierarchy in infants' attachment relationships emerged under stress with a distinctive preference for traditional mothers over traditional fathers and for traditional fathers over strangers (Bridges, Connell & Belsky, 1988; Clarke-Stewart, 1978; Lamb, 1976a).

This hierarchy in infants' attachment preference has been observed in the Strange Situation, in the presence of a scary unfamiliar object such as a clown, Big Bird, or an ambiguous stimulus. Doubt nevertheless remains concerning this order of preference which may be related to underlying factors such as the primacy of the caregiving role assumed and related involvement in child care. Thus, Russel (1983) added a note of caution when considering this hierarchy:

> Although the research has not yet been done, it seems highly likely that the differences that have been observed with regard to children turning preferentially to their mothers under conditions of stress are most likely attributable to the differences between parents in their day-to-day interactions (mothers of course are much more likely to be the primary caregivers). (p. 113)

NONTRADITIONAL PRIMARY CAREGIVING FATHER-INFANT INTERACTION

Beside the wealth of findings on traditional secondary caregiving father-infant interaction, only a few studies have examined infants' interaction with nontraditional fathers who were their infant's primary caregivers. In-depth interviews with primary caregiving fathers and their spouse were conducted in several countries including Australia (Russel, 1983), Israel (Radin, 1980), Norway (Gronseth, 1975), and the United States (Defrain, 1979). Defrain (1979) estimated that these fathers assumed approximately 46 percent of the child care, and Radin (1980) that they assumed between 41 percent to 54 percent of caregiving duties. Gronseth (1975), without specifying the exact number of hours, reported that primary caregiving fathers had an equal or greater share of child-care responsibilities than their spouse. In Russel's (1983) interviews primary caregiving fathers reported spending twenty-six hours per week in child care, which contrasted with the one hour per week traditional fathers spent with their infants.

By using a quasi-random sampling method, drawing subjects from supermarkets, Russel (1983) estimated that 10 percent of fathers in Australia were the primary caregivers of children returning from day care or preschool. This figure compares to the 7.5 percent of fathers who reported sharing caregiving duties equally with their spouse in the United States (Kotelchuck, 1976), and to the 10 percent of fathers assuming primary caregiving duties in Sweden (Gronseth, 1975). By contrast, Russel (1983) found that only 2 percent of primary caregiving fathers were taking care of infants under one year of age. Russel explains this finding by the cultural beliefs that young infants need their mother and nursing, which would conflict with fathers becoming primary caregivers of infants.

Primary caregiving fathers' attitudes toward work and child care as well as their work schedule have been found to differ from those of traditional fathers (Gronseth, 1975). Primary caregiving fathers had chosen part-time employment in order to share caregiving duties equally with their spouse. These fathers were moderately career-oriented and strongly committed to the welfare of their children. They also shared with their spouse at least 50 percent of the household chores. They wrote the checks to pay the bills, shopped, did the laundry, and prepared meals.

Further studies (Pleck & Rustad, 1980; Robinson, 1977; Russel, 1983) indicate that although mothers' employment was negatively related to the amount of housework and child care mothers performed, mothers' employment had little effect on increasing fathers' participation in child care. However, the decrease in the number of hours fathers were employed outside of the home did have a small but significant positive relation to the amount of time fathers spent on child care. Thus, the critical variable for sharing in caregiving duties was related to the amount of time fathers spent at home available to their children rather than to maternal employment.

Primary caregiving fathers have also been found to place more value on love and affection than on success and career achievement. The time fathers spent alone and fully responsible of their children resulted in greater closeness and satisfaction. Comparing past to present work and caregiving arrangements, primary caregiving fathers reported better contact with their children than in the past because they had more time and experiences with them (Gronseth, 1975; Hood & Golden, 1979). In the words of Russel (1983), "to be the person who had the sole responsibility to be the special person who was around at the critical, sensitive times appeared to contribute significantly to the change in their relationship" (p. 122). Secondary caregiving mothers reported greater enjoyment because their occupational involvement and part-time employment gave them some time away from their children and prevented them from feeling overwhelmed by them.

Aside from interview data, observational data on primary caregiving father-infant interaction are rare, and on some measures nonexistent. Two observational studies, so far, have compared primary caregiving father-infant interaction to secondary caregiving father-infant interaction and primary caregiving mother-infant interaction. In one of these studies, conducted in the United States, twelve primary and twelve secondary caregiving fathers as well as twelve primary caregiving mothers were observed in face-to-face interaction with their four-month old infants (Field, 1978). Primary caregiving fathers' behavior toward their infants has been found to have greater resemblance to that of primary caregiving mothers than to that of secondary caregiving fathers. Primary caregiving fathers exhibited approximately the same amount of grimacing, verbalization, grooming, wiping, and cleaning the baby and engaged in the same type of interactive infantile behavior as mothers did. However, they spoke less to their infants and engaged less in limb holding than did mothers. By comparison to secondary caregiving fathers, primary caregiving fathers mimicked and smiled more at their infants. They laughed less, but used higher pitched vocalization than did secondary caregiving fathers. Nevertheless, primary caregiving fathers' play style by retaining its rough-and-tumble play characteristic remained similar to that of secondary caregiving fathers.

The apparent lack of differences between primary caregiving fathers' and primary caregiving mothers' attachment behaviors toward their infant suggested that the gender of the caregiver might not be as crucial as the caregiving role assumed. On the basis of these findings, Field (1978) concluded that parental style of interaction was socially rather than biologically based.

However, Field's study suffered from several limitations. It was narrow in scope because it was based on observing the face-to-face interaction of parents with four–month old infants restrained in an infant seat. Furthermore, no operational definition was provided for the concept "primary caregiving father." The extent of primary caregiving fathers' involvement in child care was not specified, and nothing was said about subject selection. Finally, secondary caregiving mothers were not included in any comparison.

The second observational study (Frodi et al., 1983) was conducted in Sweden. Nontraditional Swedish fathers were observed interacting with their eight-, twelve-, sixteen-, and eighteen-month old infants and compared to traditional Swedish fathers interacting with infants of the same age. Fifty-one fathers were included in the study. Nontraditional fathers were characterized by their taking an average of three months' leave of absence to be spent in child care. Contrary to those of Field (1978), the results of this research indicated that the parent's gender rather than the primacy of the caregiving role accounted for differences in behavior. Regardless of whether they were classified as traditional or not, Swedish fathers were found to assume fewer caregiving duties and to be less nurturant than Swedish mothers. They neither displayed as much affection, provided as much physical contact, smiled, nor vocalized to their infants as much as mothers did. Furthermore, although traditional and nontraditional Swedish fathers alike spent more time with their infants than did U.S. fathers, they did not play as much with their infants as U.S. fathers did. Swedish fathers' play interaction was not as arousing or as pleasurable to their children as was that of U.S. fathers. Finally, the Swedish infants have been found to prefer their mother to their father by all affiliative and attachment measures regardless of whether their father was traditional or not.

Although Frodi and her colleagues (1983) had defined nontraditional fathers as those "spending on the average of three months as primary caretakers" (p. 159), the actual sample of primary caregiving fathers was selected on the basis of their *planned* rather than their *actual* involvement in child care. At the time of the first observation, that is, when the infants were eight months old, only fourteen fathers had become primary caregivers for *at least one of the three months* preceding the observation. This was indeed a very short period of time to appreciate the effect of fathers' greater involvement in child care. Furthermore, it was not specified in the study whether these nontraditional fathers had continued to assume primary caregiving duties over the course of the whole year that they were observed interacting with their infants. It is very likely that these fathers had stopped assuming primary child-care responsibilities because Swedish fathers were reported to use an average of forty-two days and mothers an average of 290 days of the eighteen months' paid leave of absence they were entitled to take (Kamerman & Kahn, 1991). As in Field's (1978) study, the extent of nontraditional fathers' involvement in play and child care was not specified. Finally, although the Frodi et al. study (1983) was longitudinal, it was conducted in a culture in which father-infant style of interaction differs qualitatively from that of the U.S. sample. The characteristic of rough-and-tumble play partnership appeared to be missing from nontraditional and traditional Swedish fathers' play style. This lack makes it hard if not impossible to extrapolate on the basis of these findings what could have been the interaction of U.S. primary caregiving fathers with their infants.

In summary, the observational studies conducted so far on primary caregiving father-infant interaction suffer from obvious limitations. They provide ambiguous and contradictory results concerning the effects of gender of the caregiver and the primacy of caregiver role on the caregiver's behavior. Furthermore, while focusing on play interaction, these studies neglected to provide a measure of responsiveness or synchrony between parents' and infants' activities. The present study was undertaken to solve these contradictions while broadening the scope of our understanding on the nature of primary caregiving father-infant interaction.

SPECIFIC RESEARCH QUESTIONS

The specific questions of this research are formulated as such:

1. What is the unique and interactive effect of the gender of the caregiver and the primacy of the caregiver role on the affiliative and attachment behaviors of parents of different gender and assuming different caregiving roles toward their infant?

2. What is the unique and interactive effect of the gender of the caregiver and the primacy of the caregiver role on the affiliative and attachment behaviors that infants display in a stress-free situation toward caregivers of different gender and assuming different caregiving roles?

3. Under stress, and when they have the choice between their father or their mother, will infants direct most attachment behaviors toward the parent of a particular gender or toward the parent who assumes primary caregiving duties?

3
Methodology

OVERVIEW

The current research was based on videotaped home observations of infants interacting with caregivers of different gender and assuming different caregiving duties. Parental interviews complemented these observations. The affiliative and attachment behaviors of parents and their infants toward each other were analyzed in order to find out the unique and interactive effects of the gender of the caregiver and the primacy of the caregiver role on caregivers' and infants' behaviors. A modified version of the Strange Situation in which infants were observed interacting with a stranger while in the presence of both of their parents provided a measure of infants' preferential attachment under stress. This chapter presents a detailed description of the subject selection and of the interview and observational procedures. The dependent variables and their behavioral definitions are examined next. Data concerning intersession and intercoder reliability are also assessed. Finally, demographic information regarding the subjects is provided.

SUBJECT SELECTION

Sample Size

Research participants were twenty-eight intact families composed of both parents and their infants. In fourteen of these families, nontraditional fathers assumed primary caregiving duties for at least half of the infant's waking hours while mothers were employed outside the home and assumed a secondary caregiving role. In the remaining fourteen families, which constituted a reference group, traditional fathers were employed full-time and assumed a secondary caregiving role while mothers were their infant's exclusive caregivers during the day.

The infants observed were mobile, that is, able to crawl or walk, and less than twenty-one months of age.[1] Attempts were made to select an equal number of male and female infants. Handicapped and otherwise developmentally impaired infants were excluded from this study. No requirement was placed on the number of additional children per family.

Recruitment of Subjects

Several approaches were adopted to recruit the subjects. The first consisted of putting announcements in all pediatricians' offices of the Capital District of New York State soliciting subjects fitting the description of primary caregiving fathers or that of primary caregiving mothers. After a two-month waiting period during which no one answered the announcements, the researcher went to malls and family entertainment sites and restaurants. Phone numbers were exchanged, but no one followed up. The obvious reason seemed to be that people were reluctant to open their doors to someone who was, after all, a stranger. Another approach had to be taken. The researcher had to be personally referred by an institution or organization. Churches, synagogues, nursery schools, as well as community and mother centers were contacted by phone. The researcher's personal appearance was sometimes requested.

Most of the subjects were recruited from referrals obtained through these agencies and from personal contacts made in the community center at which the researcher was a member. By going to the many organized family events this community center offered, the researcher could approach fathers who were taking care of their babies. The friendly and safe atmosphere of the center was conducive to gaining parents' confidence and willingness to participate in the research.

Initial phone calls were made to the prospective participants in order to explain the research procedure and obtain more information about the father's work arrangement and the way he organized his daily schedule. Questions were also asked about the infant's age and ability to crawl. Based on these phone conversations, fathers were screened into two groups. Fathers who were fulfilling primary caregiving duties for at least half of their infant's waking hours since their infant was at most seven-months old and whose spouse was employed full-time outside the home composed the group of primary caregiving fathers. A reference group, matched by education and age, was obtained from the same community sources. This group was composed of primary caregiving mothers who were their infant's exclusive caregivers during the day while their spouse was employed full-time outside the home.

Participants were requested to meet on two different days. One meeting was scheduled to last approximately twenty-five minutes. The other was expected to last at least one hour, since it included an interview with the parents after the twenty-five-minute observation. Appointments were made either in the evening around 7 P.M., generally after dinner, or on the weekend. The time elapsed between the first and second observation varied and ranged from two days to two weeks, with most of the observations occurring a week apart.

PROCEDURE

Parents' Interview

Interviews with parents were designed to obtain demographic information concerning the parents' age, education, employment, and child-rearing practices. Some questions in the interview guide asked parents about their child-care arrangements during the week and on weekends. Other questions asked them whether they used the services of a babysitter, and if they did, for how many hours a week. Parents were also asked about the way they shared the caregiving tasks of bathing, feeding, diapering, and putting baby to sleep when they were both home. They were asked for how long they had adopted the present child-care arrangement, why they had chosen this type of arrangement, what was the previous child-care arrangement, and whether they had considered day care as an option. Finally, they were asked whether they had been camera conscious and whether being videotaped had changed the way they normally behaved with their infant, and if it had, what changes had occurred. (The parents' interview guide is reproduced in Appendix A).

Materials

The materials used in this study were minimal. The infant's own toys were placed on the living room floor, and two chairs were needed for the last episode of the observation. Parents were asked to interact freely with their infants as much as possible without leaving the living room. All parent-infant interactions were videotaped with a hand-held 8mm Camcorder. The portability and small size of this camcorder allowed unobtrusive observation.

Observation Procedure

Each family was videotaped twice for twenty-five minutes when both parents were at home and when the child was awake, and preferably after a nap. Each observation was composed of three semi-structured episodes.

1. During *episode 1*, one of the parents was observed interacting alone with the infant for ten minutes.

2. During *episode 2*, the other parent was observed interacting alone with the infant for ten minutes.

3. During *episode 3*, the infant was observed interacting with a friendly stranger for five minutes. Parents were seated across each other on chairs at opposite sides of the stranger who was interacting with the infant in the center.

   a. A female stranger (the researcher) greeted the infant in whatever area of the living room the infant was located.

   b. The stranger offered a toy to the infant and invited the infant to enter into a reciprocal game. The infant was allowed to roam freely on the living room floor.

   c. After two or three minutes, the stranger picked up the infant. Parents were instructed to remain in their respective seats and to direct no specific attention to the infant while the infant was being picked up and then put back on the floor.

Infants were observed at each step of this procedure, and especially while and after they were picked up by the stranger in order to assess toward which parent would most attachment behaviors be directed under increasing levels of stress.

Episode 3 constitutes a standardized five-minute modified version of the Strange Situation developed by Stevenson and Lamb (1979). This procedure was chosen because of its superiority to that of Ainsworth. In Ainsworth's Strange Situation (Ainsworth et al., 1978) parents and stranger constantly appear and disappear from the infant and hence may induce an extraordinary level of stress. This situation often results in the observation of "the strange behavior of children in a strange situation with strange adults for the briefest periods of time" (Bronfenbrenner, 1977). By observing infants in their home environment and by asking parents to remain in the room during all infant-stranger interaction, the present procedure was expected to be stressful, but not bizarre to the infant, and thus to yield ecologically valid data.

In order to balance the primacy of appearance of the parents in the sample, the order in which each parent interacted with the infant was reversed at the second videotaped session. The parent who had interacted first in episode 1 of the first session, interacted second in episode 2 of the second session, and vice versa. Similarly, the seating arrangement of the parents in episode 3 was reversed in the first and second videotaped sessions. The parent sitting to the right of the stranger during the first session of episode 3 sat to the left of the stranger during the second session, and vice versa. This rotation was expected to neutralize any set in the infant's behavior pattern. The infant's tendency to always go, for instance, to the parent sitting to the right of the researcher would be counterbalanced by switching the parents' sitting position in the first and the second videotaped sessions.

Dependent Variables and Coding Procedures

All videotaped interactions of parents with their infants were analyzed into dependent measures of affiliation and attachment behaviors that parents and infants exhibited toward each other under stressful and nonstressful conditions.

1. The first dependent measure, *Parent's Affiliative Behavior*, was analyzed into the following behaviors: holds, looks, talks to child, plays with books, plays games, and plays rough-and-tumble.

2. The second dependent measure, *Parent's Attachment Behavior*, was analyzed into the following behaviors: caregives and displays affection.

3. The third dependent measure, *Infant's Affiliative Behavior*, was analyzed into the following behaviors: resists parent's activity, initiates an activity, involves parent in activity, plays together, plays alone, looks, laughs, and vocalizes.

4. The fourth dependent measure, *Infant's Attachment Behavior*, was analyzed into the following behaviors: displays affection, moves away, explores objects, approaches, in proximity, and clings.

5. The fifth dependent measure, *Infant's Affiliative Behavior under Stress*, was analyzed into the following behaviors: joins stranger's activity, ignores stranger's activity, plays alone, smiles or laughs, and vocalizes.

6. The sixth dependent measure, *Infant's Attachment Behaviors under Stress*, was analyzed into the following behaviors: in proximity of father or mother, approaches father or mother, looks at father or mother, turns body toward mother or father, resists father or mother, and physical contact with father or mother.

7. The *Indicators of Stress* were the following: stranger holding the infant, whining, screaming.

(The behavioral definitions of each one of the behaviors specified for the dependent measures of affiliation and attachment under nonstressful and stressful conditions may be found in Appendix B.)

Each ten-minute interaction episode was time sampled into thirty twenty-second intervals. The dependent measures were recorded once for each twenty-second interval in which they were observed to occur. Records for fathers, mothers, and strangers were kept distinct. To allow for accurate coding of the numerous behaviors observed, each twenty-second interaction interval was further broken down into five seconds of viewing time and fifteen seconds of coding time. Viewing and coding time segments were cued with a tape recorder. The pattern was as follows: look 1 (five seconds), code 1 (fifteen seconds), look 2, code 2, look 3, code 3, . . . look 30, code 30. (The coding sheets for parents' and infants' affiliative and attachment behaviors are reproduced in Appendix C.)

VALIDITY AND RELIABILITY

The influence of the observer's presence on parent-infant interaction, the reliability of the observations, and the reliability of the coding had to be addressed in order to guarantee valid and reliable data.

Observer Influence

The mere presence of an observer was likely to influence parents' behavior. Parents could become overly self-conscious when observed and modify their normal way of behaving. The influence of the observer on parent-infant interaction has been found to be more pronounced in laboratory than in home observations. For instance, informed and noninformed mothers were found to behave differently with their five-year old children when they were observed through a one-way mirror. Informed mothers structured their activities, were more verbal, and used more positive verbal behavior with their children than did noninformed mothers (Zegiob, Arnold & Forehand, 1975).

In the current study, the presence of the camera and that of the observer were expected to influence parents' behavior in the direction of greater social desirability. Parents were expected to exhibit less negative behaviors such as yelling at the baby or at the spouse, less discipline, more leniency and acceptance, as well as more interaction with their infants. Thus, several safeguards have been adopted to counteract the influence of an observer. The first was to guarantee research participants their anonymity: their identity, names, or addresses would not appear in any published material.

The second was to obtain good rapport with the parents. For this purpose, up to five phone calls were made before the observations. To reduce the problem of social desirability, it was emphasized that the primary interest was to observe and videotape the usual way infants interact with their parents (Lamb, 1980; Pedersen, 1980).

Explaining the purpose of the research was another strategy to lower the parents' apprehension. However, explaining too much of the purpose could have increased the number of socially desirable behaviors. For instance, telling the subjects that the goal of the research was to find out how much their infants were attached to them could have made parents behave less naturally. Using Belsky's (1980) wording, parents were told that the primary interest was "to learn about the infant's everyday world" (p. 91). This phrase, which did not reveal too much about the purpose of the research, moved the focus of the observation from the parents onto the child, while making parents less self-conscious, less apprehensive, and more at ease.

On the days of actual observations, parents were told to interact as they usually do with their infants. The wording was very important. "Typical" was not used because it could have misled parents to think about what was typical and what was not. Parents were told to behave as they usually do, but at the same time they were instructed to do so by interacting for ten minutes with their infant and while in their living room. Interview questions aimed at finding out whether these were the usual conditions under which the parent and the infant interacted together.

In past research, the time period estimated to make the parents feel at ease was determined to be eighty minutes (Lamb, 1980; Pedersen, 1980). However, participants were not instructed, as in the present research, to remain in their living room. As a result, the researcher was often left observing nothing while sitting in the living room. By condensing the observation time to twenty-five minutes and instructing parents to remain in the living room for that period of time, the present study was expected to prevent the child from being fatigued and the parents from being bored, and thus to allow for more representative interaction.

Camera Obtrusiveness

Natural observation seems to be the ideal medium of research with young children who do not use behavioral camouflage or concealment. If the observers are passive and behaving routinely, their presence is often unobtrusive to the child (Goodwin & Driscoll, 1980). However, the presence of the camera could have affected the natural behavior of children. From trial sessions, the researcher noticed that children liked to pose in front of the camera and that any looking or smiling at the child while videotaping was an invitation for such behavior. Connolly and Smith (1972), who made the same observation, concluded that whereas observers' friendliness was likely to increase children's interaction with them, observers' passivity assured unobtrusiveness. Thus, videotaping was conducted while the researcher maintained a neutral face without expression and avoided eye contact with the child. This reduced the child's attempt to interact with the camerawoman and induced the child to forget about the camera.

To check the representativeness of the observations, parents were asked whether being videotaped had changed their behavior or that of their infants. Most of the parents (88%) reported that they had at first felt somewhat camera conscious, but after a while they had forgotten the camera. Some parents (42%) commented that they had initiated more activities than they normally would during the time they had been observed and that they had been more directive than usual. For example, a secondary caregiving mother reported: "It made me self-conscious in the sense that I normally do not interact with her so deliberately. If she was in the room and playing, I might just sit in the room and watch her play. I might be less interactive."

Normally, parents would let their children roam throughout the house and entertain themselves without interfering. Direction would come upon children's request. Parents also reported that their children would let them know when they needed personal attention either by crying or clinging.

By contrast, only a few parents (8%) mentioned that they had reduced their interaction with their infants while being videotaped. They felt that they had looked and talked less than usual to their children. The remaining parents (50%) felt that they had behaved normally with their infants.

Several fathers also reported that they had engaged less in rough-and-tumble play than they normally would have because they had to interact with their infants for ten minutes. Rough-and-tumble play was engaged in for much shorter periods of time and was judged to be quite exhausting to the infant.

Reliability of the Measures

A series of observations could have allowed for a better estimate of infants' typical behavior and thus increased the reliability of the measures. However, parents were not likely to let the researcher intrude upon their private lives too frequently. Furthermore, infants grow up quickly, and what might have been a typical behavior for infants at three months of age could become atypical at five months of age. Nevertheless, a single observation was not sufficient to ensure reliability of the measures. Parents were therefore requested to allow two videotaped sessions. Scheduled a short period of time apart—a few days to two weeks—these two sessions were expected to achieve stability and representativeness.

Intersession Reliability

The reliability of parents' and infants' behavior under stressful and nonstressful conditions has been assessed. Product moment correlation between the behaviors coded in sessions 1 and 2 was the statistic used in the computation of intersession reliability. The reliability of parents' affiliative and attachment behaviors toward their infant was examined first. The frequencies of most parents' affiliative and attachment behaviors—holds, talks, reads, plays with books, plays conventional games, rough-and-tumble, and displays affection—were found to correlate significantly from one session to the next ($p<.01$). The coefficient of correlation for these measures ranged from .25 to .59 and averaged to .43 (Appendix D, Table D.1).

The frequency of looking has not been found consistent between sessions because it depended on the seating arrangement of the parent and the infant and the type of activity in which they were engaged. Although most of the time parents looked and talked to their infants, looking was not coded when the child was not in the parent's field of vision. This occurred when the child sat on the parent's lap while the parent was reading to the child or when the parent gave the child a ride on his or her back.

The reliability of infants' behavior toward their parents was assessed next under nonstressful and stressful conditions. Except for display of affection, all other infants' affiliative and attachment behaviors under nonstressful conditions—resists parent, initiates activity, involves parent, plays together, plays alone, looks at parent, smiles or laughs, vocalizes, displays affection, moves away, explores, approaches, in proximity, and clings—were found to correlate significantly ($p<.01$) from one session to the next. The coefficient of correlation for these measures ranged from .28 to .59 and averaged to .46 (Appendix D, Tables D.2 and D.3).

Finally, under stressful conditions most infants' attachment behaviors toward their parents—proximity maintaining, looking, turning body toward, and physical contact with father or mother—were found to be very reliable and to correlate significantly ($\underline{p}$<.01) from one session to the next. The coefficient of correlation ranged from .39 to .75 and averaged to .57 (Appendix D, Table D.4).

The measures of approaching mother and approaching father were not found to be reliable between sessions. A possible explanation for this lack of consistency is that these measures were complementary to the measures of maintaining proximity to the attachment figure. Thus, when taken separately, each one of these measures could vary from one session to another, but the frequency of these measures combined together remained consistent between the two sessions.

The frequency with which the stranger picked up or held the infant also varied from one session to the next depending on the level of stress the infant was judged to experience. For instance, when an infant was judged in session 1 to be under a lot of stress he or she was not, often, picked up by the stranger. However, if in session 2 the same infant was judged to be less stressed, he or she was picked up or held by the stranger until some kind of resistance was felt.

Intercoder Reliability

Reliability of the Observations

Another issue to be addressed was that of the reliability of the observation. Except for Field's study (1978), no other research on father-infant interaction had videotaped its observations. A trained observer usually coded his or her observations directly while viewing the interaction (Belsky, 1980; Lamb 1980; Pedersen, 1980). Bias and distortion were hard to prevent. The presence of a second observer was not permissible because the presence of one observer had been judged obtrusive enough. To allow for a second observer's account of the interaction, other visits were usually scheduled with additional families. The interreliability of the coding was assessed by correlating the coding of the first coder with that of the second coder.

In the current study, by videotaping the interaction rather than relying on the observer's judgment, the problem of bias or distortion did not arise at the level of observation but was postponed to the coding stage. Nevertheless, the problem of camera obtrusiveness was considered to be less severe than the interference of an observer constantly murmuring into a microphone of the tape recorder or keypunching codes on a keyboard. Another advantage of videotaping was that all the material remained perpetually available to the coders. Two coders could watch as long as it was needed to code the material and check the reliability of the coding.

Reliability of the Coding

Two coders were trained by using transcripts other than those they had to code for a check of interreliability until they consistently achieved a level of agreement above 80 percent on all behavior categorizations. Categories for which such a level of agreement had not been achieved were eliminated. This was the case of parent smiling, positive talk to the child, teaching, parent playing with toys, and tickling. Data was coded according to the remaining behavioral categories.

Reliability of the coding was determined by comparing the coding of coder 1 with the coding of coder 2 on 10 percent of the sessions. Since each one of the twenty-eight families in this study was videotaped twice, the interreliability check was based on six videotapes randomly chosen from a total of fifty-six videotaped sessions. Each of the six videotaped sessions was viewed three times. The first time a check on the reliability of the coding of parents' affiliative and attachment behaviors toward their infants was performed. The second viewing was designed to check the reliability of the coding of the infants' affiliative and attachment behaviors toward their parents in nonstressful situations, and the third was to check the reliability of the coding of infants' behavior under stress.

Reliability of the Coding of Parents' Behavior toward Their Infants. After a six-hour training period, two coders met twice to view each time three videotaped sessions. In each of these sessions, fathers interacted with their infant for ten minutes, then mothers interacted with their infant for ten minutes. The percentage of intercoder agreement was computed for all affiliative and attachment behaviors that the parents displayed toward their infant as observed agreement (P), which does not take into account chance occurrence, and as Cohen's kappa (K), which corrects for chance occurrence (Sattler, 1992, p. 514).

The percentage (P) of observed intercoder agreement was found to be very high and to range from 92 to 100 percent for all parents' behaviors. Percentage agreement (K) computed with Cohen's kappa formula was somewhat lower but remained high. It ranged from 80 to 100 percent for all dependent measures of parents' affiliative and attachment behavior. (The coding sheet for parents' affiliative and attachment behavior is reproduced in Appendix C1.)

Reliability of the Coding of Infants' Behavior in a Nonstressful Situation.
A second analysis was conducted to check the reliability of the coding of the
infants' affiliative and attachment behaviors toward their parents in a
nonstressful situation. The same procedure as the one mentioned above was
used. Two coders met twice to view, once more, the same six twenty-minute
videotaped sessions while focusing on the infants' behaviors in episodes 1
and 2. Infants were observed interacting with their fathers for ten minutes,
then with their mothers for ten minutes. The same audiotape dividing these
ten minutes into thirty twenty-second periods was played. At each period
the two coders looked at the videotape for five seconds and coded for fifteen
seconds while the videotape continued to play. (The coding sheet for
infants' affiliative and attachment behavior is reproduced in Appendix C2.)

As was the case with parents' behavior, percentage (P) of intercoder
observed agreement for infants' behaviors in a nonstressful situation was
found to be high and to range from 92 to 100 percent. When chance
occurrence was included into the computation of reliability by using
Cohen's kappa formula (K), intercoder agreement was reduced but remained
high. It ranged from 80 to 97 percent and reached 86 percent agreement for
most of infants' affiliative and attachment behaviors coded under
nonstressful conditions.

Reliability of the Coding of Infants' Behavior in a Stressful Situation.
The third interreliability analysis aimed at checking the reliability of the
coding of the infants' affiliative and attachment behaviors under stress. Two
coders met once more to view the third episode of the same six videotaped
sessions, each of which lasted approximately five minutes. Infants were
viewed interacting with a stranger following a modified version of the
Strange Situation. The same coding procedure was used as before. (The
coding sheet for infants' behaviors in a stressful situation is reproduced in
Appendix C3.)

As in the two previous interreliability analyses, percentage of observed
intercoder agreement (P) for infants' behaviors in a Strange Situation was
high and ranged from 84 to 100 percent. When computed with Cohen's
kappa formula, intercoder agreement was reduced but remained high. It
ranged from 78 to 100 percent and remained above 88 percent for most of
the infants' behaviors coded in a stressful situation.

DEMOGRAPHIC INFORMATION

Demographic information was based on parental interview data.
Information about nontraditional families composed of primary caregiving
fathers and secondary caregiving mothers and their infant, and about more

traditional families composed of secondary caregiving fathers and primary caregiving mothers and their infant, was kept distinct.

Information about Infants

The gender and age distributions of the infant participants from traditional and nontraditional families were similar. The sample of infants from nontraditional families was composed of six males and eight females, that from traditional families of eight males and six females.

The age of the infants ranged from eight to twenty-one months in both types of families. The mean age of the infants in nontraditional families was thirteen months, and the modal age was ten months. The mean age of infants in traditional families was thirteen and a half months, and the modal age was eleven months.

The number of children (infant participants plus siblings) per family ranged from one to five and averaged 1.79 in each family type. Seven infant participants from nontraditional families and four infant participants from traditional families had no siblings. Finally, except for one infant from a nontraditional family who had a newborn sister, all other infant participants from both family types were the youngest children in their families.

Information about Parents

Parents' Age

The age of the parents in both family types ranged from twenty-three to over forty years of age, with mean and median ages falling within the thirty-five to thirty-nine age bracket. There did not seem to be a relationship between age and the caregiving role assumed.

Parents' Education

Educational level was distributed evenly through all parents in both groups. Parents in both family types had a high school diploma and 93 percent of them had a college degree. Four out of the seven parents who did not have a college degree were younger than twenty-five years old and came from nontraditional families. The three other parents reported having some college education but no degree. (See Table E.1 of Appendix E.)

Employment

The employment patterns varied according to the caregiving role assumed and the family type. Table 3.1 presents a frequency breakdown of the number of working hours for the various categories of caregivers.

Table 3.1
Hours of Employment per Week: Frequency Count

	Prim	Fa	Sec	Mo	Sec	Fa	Prim	Mo
Hours	n	Pct	n	Pct	n	Pct	n	Pct
None	3	21%	0	0%	0	0%	11	79%
10–16/wk	2	14%	0	0%	0	0%	3	21%
16–24/wk	6	43%	3	21%	0	0%	0	0%
25–35/wk	3	21%	3	21%	1	7%	0	0%
36–40/wk	0	0%	8	57%	9	64%	0	0%
>40/wk	0	0%	0	0%	4	29%	0	0%
Total	14	99%*	14	99%*	14	100%	14	100%

Notes: Prim Fa = Primary Caregiving Fathers; Second Fa = Secondary Caregiving Fathers; Prim Mo = Primary Caregiving Mothers; Second Mo = Secondary Caregiving Mothers. *Due to rounding error some percentages do not sum to 100%.

As indicated in Table 3.1, in nontraditional and traditional families alike, the parent (father or mother) assuming secondary caregiving duties was employed full-time outside the home. By contrast, the employment pattern of the parent assuming primary caregiving duties varied according to the family type. In nontraditional families, 79 percent of the primary caregiving fathers worked outside the home, whereas in traditional families only 21 percent of the primary caregiving mothers did.

Another difference between the employment pattern of primary and secondary caregiving fathers was the number of working hours. Most of the primary caregiving fathers (79%) worked part-time, that is, less than thirty-five hours per week. By contrast, most of the secondary caregiving fathers (93%) worked full-time, that is, more than thirty-six hours per week.

Profession

The primary caregiving fathers in this sample were self-employed and/or professionals. Four primary caregiving fathers were attorneys, two others were Ph.D. students, and another was a college professor. Two of them were business owners of a restaurant and movie theater, and another was a self-employed architect. Finally, two other primary caregiving fathers worked the night shift as supervisors, one in a food factory and the other in an institution for retarded people. The three unemployed primary caregiving fathers had also been professionals or business owners in the past. One of them was an architect who had recently moved to the area, the two others were a carpenter and a business administrator who had taken a leave a absence to take care of their infant.

Having flexible working hours, primary caregiving fathers could plan a schedule that allowed them to take care of their infant during the day. The way these fathers planned their days was sometimes very complicated. For instance, the primary caregiving father who was a food factory supervisor left for work at 10 P.M., and finished work at 10 A.M. He would then drive to the babysitter's house to pick up his infant who had been dropped there at 8 A.M. by his mother on her way to work. When asked when he had the chance to sleep, this father mentioned that his job required on and off supervision and that he was allowed to sleep in between. Another primary caregiving father explained, "I would go to my office at 3 A.M. in the morning and stay there until noon, and then she would go to her office at noon and stay there until 5 P.M."

Most of the secondary caregiving fathers were also self-employed and/or professionals. Two of these fathers were dentists, two others were physicians (one a psychiatrist), and still two others were engineers. One secondary caregiving father was a business manager, three others were business owners, and another was a Ph.D. student in a polytechnical institute. One secondary caregiving father was a computer scientist, another a corrections officer, and still another a song writer and performer. The nature of secondary caregiving fathers' professions usually required dealing with people as patients or customers during business hours and thus did not allow them too much leeway in scheduling their working hours.

Secondary caregiving mothers were professionals but generally not self-employed. The breakdown of their professions runs as follows: one psychologist, one computer scientist, one beauty salon owner, one student in nursing, one supervisor in a facility for retarded people, one economist, one professor, two teachers, one lawyer, one architect, one pharmacist, two executive secretaries.

Most of the primary caregiving mothers did not work outside the home. They had abandoned their careers as day-care or school teachers or as nurses in order to take care of their infant full-time. Two of them had continued to work less than eight hours a week. One was an editor at home, the other worked two hours a week as a teacher of a toddler group and brought her infant with her to work. In summary, by employment and education, most of the parents in this study were middle-class college graduates and professionals.

NOTE

1. This age has been chosen because the Strange Situation procedure has been found to lack validity and reliability for infants older than 20 months.

4

Results

The results chapter is divided into two parts. The first part presents the data obtained from interviews with nontraditional and traditional parents concerning the child-care arrangements they had adopted. The second part focuses on observational data. Codification of the observational data into behavioral categories and subsequent statistical analyses have been performed to provide answers to specific research questions concerning the unique and interactive effects of the caregiver gender and caregiving role on parent-infant interaction.

INTERVIEW DATA

Results of the interview data are presented in tabular form and by quoting the various caregivers. In order to preserve the anonymity of the subjects, all names were replaced by fictitious pseudonyms. Each quote is identified by Primary Father, Secondary Mother, Secondary Father, or Primary Mother, depending on the category to which the caregiver quoted belonged.

CHILD-CARE ARRANGEMENTS

The child-care arrangements adopted by nontraditional and traditional families varied slightly since the majority of primary caregiving fathers worked outside the home, whereas the majority of primary caregiving mothers did not. In nontraditional families, most of primary caregiving fathers (65%) used the regular services of a babysitter during the day for short periods of time and up to fifteen hours per week. In traditional families, primary caregiving mothers were, during the day, their infant's exclusive caregivers. Nevertheless, traditional families would occasionally hire a babysitter to go out at night, approximately every other weekend.

Table 4.1
Duration of Present Child-Care Arrangement:
Frequency Count

	Nontrad Families		Trad Families	
	n	Pct	n	Pct
Always	5	36%	14	100%
Since Baby 4–8 Months	9	64%	0	0%
Since Baby > 8 Months	0	0%	0	0%
	14	100%	14	100%

Note: Nontrad = Nontraditional; Trad = Traditional.

Another difference that was noted between traditional and nontraditional families was related to the length of time since the actual child-care arrangement had been adopted. As indicated in Table 4.1, all primary caregiving mothers, as opposed to only 36 percent of the primary caregiving fathers, had always been their infant's primary caregivers. All other nontraditional fathers (64%) had become primary caregivers when their infants were between four and eight months of age. When that was the case, secondary caregiving mothers (57%) had obtained a maternity leave of absence, generally lasting from six weeks to eight months, to take care of their infants after birth. The other 7 percent of secondary caregiving mothers who had not taken a maternity leave of such length had arranged for a babysitter to come to their home up until the time fathers had become their infant's primary caregivers.

CHOOSING A PARTICULAR CHILD-CARE ARRANGEMENT

Attitude toward Child Care and Day Care

Several factors combine to explain why nontraditional and traditional families examined in the present study had adopted the child-care arrangement in which one of the parents stayed at home with the infant. Parents' attitude toward child care was one of the factors influencing the choice of child-care arrangement. Parents in both family types perceived taking care of their infant to be the parent's responsibility. However, although the same arguments were presented by nontraditional and traditional parents, the wording they used was different. Primary caregiving mothers usually expressed themselves with the first person singular pronoun "I," whereas primary caregiving fathers and secondary caregiving mothers expressed their arguments with the plural pronoun "we." The difference in the use of pronouns reflected from the onset a difference in what they meant by "taking care of the baby," and suggested that primary caregiving mothers did not consider fathers to be responsible for child care during the day, whereas secondary caregiving mothers did.

> *I* felt *I* had to be around her. Well *I* am new at this. (*Primary Mother*)

> *We* thought about it for a long time. So *we* were more comfortable that way. *We* decided that if *we* could ever do it in such a way, *we* wouldn't have to send our children to day care. (*Primary Father*)

Some parents were not really sure why they did not opt for another alternative, but they felt that one of the parents had to stay with the child.

> I was not sure about it, but I felt pretty strongly that one of *us* should stay with him for about a year. I am glad that we did. (*Secondary Mother*)

Other parents mentioned their own psychological needs and those of their infant. Some mothers felt that the separation from their infant was too hard to bear:

> I could not stay apart from him for eight hours and then see him all red in the face and he cried and cried. (*Primary Mother*)

> I would have had a real hard time going back to work if I had put him in day care when he was two or three months old. I know people do it all the time. But we had the flexibility not to do it and we thought that it was best not to. (*Secondary Mother*)

Some parents reported that infants need constancy of care and closeness with their mother:

> For the moment I think that's the best thing for the children . . . and me.

I feel it is maybe a sacrifice; the word is maybe too strong. It is important enough that I . . . I feel I have to be with them. (*Primary Mother*)

She needs the same people around her. (*Primary Mother*)

It is not the right philosophy. I believe that for the first three years of life the child should be very close to his mother and father. (*Primary Mother*)

One mother stated that infants need their parents to develop trust:

I think that psychologically to gain trust between parent and child it is absolutely necessary to be a primary caregiver. *I* think it is a mistake to put the child in day care. You should stay with the child for the first couple of years. (*Primary Mother*)

Another reported that infants also need individual attention:

It seems to be the time when they need undivided attention. You know at this age they start to get attached. (*Primary Mother*)

In both family types, parents' attitude toward day care prevented them from considering this alternative as an option. Some parents did not know exactly why they should not put their infant in day care, but they did not feel comfortable with the idea. Other parents believed that day care could not satisfy their infant's psychological and physical needs. Infants needed a special relationship and bonding with their mother in order to develop properly. In the words of some primary caregiving mothers:

I cannot or should not knock down day care, especially being an educator. It is good, but the mother-child relationship is an important relationship, especially in the beginning, in the first year. (*Primary Mother*)

I personally would not put my child in day care because there is no bonding, and if you do not bond when you are little, how are you going to bond later! (*Primary Mother*)

I feel that there is no substitute for your own parents and home environment. I do not think that day-care people can ever love the child as much as the mother. (*Primary Mother*)

One parent stated that day care could not provide the individualized attention or the one-to-one relationship that infants needed:

> The reason is that I would not be secure in knowing that they are as attentive to his needs as I could be, or that they are treating him as well as I would. (*Primary Mother*)

Other parents mentioned that they could not trust day-care professionals and feared that in day care their infant would be neglected:

> I worked in day care. I saw a lot of neglect. They were not as gentle as they should be and I did not like that. . . . We wanted to raise him. (*Secondary Mother*)

> I would rather wait that my children get older so that they can communicate to me the things that happen. I do not really trust them. My mother told me to never trust anybody with your children. (*Primary Mother*)

Still others parents pictured their infant abandoned in a corner of the day-care center and miserable:

> I get mad at her sometimes too you know, but I think nobody will pick her up and try to take care of her needs as her mom. If someone else took care of her, they would put her in a corner and let her cry. (*Secondary Mother*)

Also, parents were concerned that infants at this age may catch several diseases:

> We did not want him to be exposed to all kinds of illnesses, and we wanted him to get some personal attention. (*Primary Father*)

> We had some friends who had their children in day care, and all three of them developed Guardia. You know that microorganism that gets into the intestines. Their baby was sick for a year. You know it is from people changing diapers without washing their hands. (*Primary Mother*)

Some parents reported that even the directors of day-care centers were not sure that day care was such a good thing for young infants:

We were not sure of Ronald's schedule, and we had the opportunity to put him in one when he was five months old. This person who was the director of the program said, "I would not put my baby there." She said, "It is a wonderful program, the children are well taken care of, but it is better if they are at home." (*Secondary Mother*)

Actually the people in the program said, "You know, this is not really a good program for babies. It is better for kids who can walk, it is right for toddlers." (*Primary Father*)

A primary caregiving father argued that there was really no reason to leave his baby with a babysitter for the entire day:

I did not want to leave him all day at the babysitter. Because there is no reason to do it. I mean there are days when I need to do things so he could have stayed at the babysitter, but generally speaking, I am not doing that much so that I can't take care of him.

Motivation to Take Care of the Baby

Another factor determining the choice of child-care arrangement was motivation. Primary caregiving fathers and primary caregiving mothers were highly motivated to take care of their infant. Because of their age, some primary caregiving mothers and fathers argued that they might never again have the opportunity to experience parenthood. It seemed to them a totally new adventure that they wanted to enjoy:

I am an older mother. Personally, I may never have this chance again. I want to be here to enjoy it. So that is why I am doing this. (*Primary Mother*)

It got close to the time when Arleen finished her maternity leave. And one day we were driving home. We said we were just not comfortable with the idea of leaving the baby with someone else—and I knew there will not be any more chances to do it, so I decided to take a plunge. (*Primary Father*)

Another couple (*Primary Mother, Secondary Father*) remembered the many years they had to wait to have a baby:

Mother: I always thought if I ever was going to have a child, I wanted to enjoy the first year.

Father: We did not have children for a long time.

Mother: We waited eight years before we had Jenny.

Spending time with their children when they were young seemed very important to many primary caregiving fathers:

I used to work twelve to fourteen hours a day. I wanted to take care of the kids. I wanted to spend more time with my kids. (*Primary Father*)

We talked about it. It was something I wanted to do if it was allowable. I wanted to spend time with the baby when he was little. (*Primary Father*)

It was important for both of us to be with him. We wanted to see him grow. (*Primary Father*)

I think with Nancy that whatever we do in terms of a job, this is something we will never get back again. I have the rest of my life to work. (*Primary Father*)

Beliefs about Women's and Men's Role in Infant Care

Nontraditional and traditional parents alike held the common belief that infant care is the responsibility of the parents. However, their beliefs about who should care for the baby during the day differed. In traditional families, primary caregiving mothers seemed to have rejected stereotypical beliefs about men's role or lack of role in infant care. Nevertheless, they continued to adopt a traditional view concerning the role of women while toning their arguments down by using the word "job" rather than "role."

Since their spouse worked all day, sometimes more than forty hours a week, primary caregiving mothers believed that their job was to caregive and perform the household chores. Whether they liked it or not, they considered this arrangement fair:

Obviously, I have to take care of them all day since he is at work. (*Primary Mother*)

He is busy with his job and then there are time constraints. So I am home. I have to do more of the child care—that's my job. (*Primary Mother*)

It's going to seem really old fashioned: If I was working outside the home and the children were in day care, I suppose I would want things to be different than the way they are now, which is basically that I do the majority of the upkeep and the running of the household. (*Primary Mother*)

The situation we have now is that I do most of the child care. But that's my job, and it works out well that way. . . . And I think he does enough. There are a lot of jobs I hate, but I am sure that he does a lot of jobs at work that he hates doing too. We have to do them. (*Primary Mother*)

All but one primary caregiving mother interviewed in this study had rejected the traditional belief that fathers were not capable of assuming complete responsibility of their infant's care. The exception argued that there were innate biological differences between mothers and fathers evidenced by childbearing and nursing that necessarily implied that mothers were programmed by nature to assume primary caregiving responsibilities.

Even if I had a career that would pay as well as Joe's does, I would not want to change the situation—that we would have to take care of her 50/50. I am not saying that a father cannot do as well a caregiving job, but I believe that God gave us breasts and milk and food in our body for a reason. (*Primary Mother*)

No secondary caregiving mother felt that child care was her exclusive domain or that fathers were less competent than mothers. One of these mothers clearly expressed her anxiety about taking care of the baby by herself and how much more competent her spouse had been while assuming various primary caregiving tasks:

I was very comfortable that he was taking care of the baby. He was more patient than I am. He just seemed to know more. I never knew anything about babies. I rarely babysat and I learned a lot from him. He taught me what to do.

Another secondary caregiving mother stressed how much easier the tasks of putting the baby to sleep and comforting the baby seemed when they were assumed by her spouse (Primary Father):

Mother: Alan is used to being comforted by his father, so he falls asleep in his arms more easily than he falls asleep in my arms. He is comfortable with me, but when it comes to getting him to sleep, Bruce does it better.

Interviewer: And when the baby cries, who does the comforting?

Father: We both try to, but if I pick him up, he will calm down right away. This is not as true for Beth. This is only natural because I am spending more time with him, he focuses on me somewhat more.

Other secondary caregiving mothers expressed with great pride that their spouse assumed more child-care responsibilities than they did:

It's a good thing that I nurse the baby because he does everything else! (*Secondary Mother*)

The only thing he does not do is cut his nails. (*Secondary Mother*)

Another secondary mother noted:

I think it is great because it gives him an opportunity that a lot of men do not have.

Beliefs about Nursing

Despite divergent beliefs about women's roles, mothers in nontraditional and traditional families alike stressed the value of nursing their infants. The caregiving role assumed (primary or secondary), and related employment outside of the home, did not greatly affect mothers' decision to nurse their baby. All but one primary caregiving mother and all but three secondary caregiving mothers had nursed or were still nursing their infant at the time of the interview. In this context, only one primary caregiving mother argued that the caregiving role assumed ought to be determined by the ability to nurse.

I believe that as long as the baby is nursing she needs to be with her mother. Therefore, there should be only one primary caregiver, and I think ideally it should be the nursing mother.

While some primary caregiving mothers had nursed their infants more than one year, the majority of primary and secondary caregiving mothers nursed their infants between three to twelve months. The difference noted between these two groups of mothers was in the frequency of nursing. Primary caregiving mothers could nurse their infants on demand, whereas secondary caregiving mothers could not. Given their employment outside of the home, secondary caregiving mothers had either to express milk throughout the day or limit nursing to mornings and evenings.

For some mothers, expressing milk did not present a problem. A secondary mother answered to the interviewer's argument in the following manner:

> *Interviewer:* Some people claim that working and nursing don't go together.
>
> *Mother:* What we did is that I rented an electric breast pump for six months or so, and so I would express milk at work and put it in a cooler. I would bring it back home after work and then freeze it. We had that whole routine down so John could have milk for the day to feed the baby.

For other mothers, expressing milk was a terrible ordeal. A primary caregiving mother shared with us how hard it was for her, until she decided to take a maternity leave:

> I worked for four weeks, and it was a total nightmare. You did not get to socialize during lunch or during any little break. I could not socialize. I was sitting in the bathroom pumping. So I applied for a two-year maternity leave, and they gave it to me.

Still others did not give up nursing in spite of the pressure they encountered at work:

> I felt pressured when I worked at Riverside Hospital. Especially in my first year I got a lot of pressure to stay evenings to run a head injury group. And I had to say, "No. I am not going to do it because my time with my baby is more important." *They did not seem to understand that my baby is nursing and I am not going to change her nursing schedule for this.* And I saw the seeds of discontent early, and it made me realize more why I wanted to go into private practice. (*Secondary Mother*)

Level of Education and Exposure to Child-Care Innovations

Several studies (Ericksen, Yancey & Ericksen, 1979; Russel, 1983) have indicated women's level of education as a crucial factor in determining the degree of fathers' participation in child care. The explanation provided was that women's greater level of education gives them equal status and decision power in the division of labor between spouses. In the current study, mothers' level of education was high. All but two mothers held a college degree, with most of the secondary caregiving mothers holding at least a master's degree (Appendix E, Table E.1).

A secondary caregiving mother noted her superior status by the seating arrangements at dinner table:

> When we were both working, when we came home I cooked and James sat on this chair [she points to the chair she is sitting on] next to the baby during the meal. Now James does the cooking and I sit on this chair next to the baby and I feed the baby, although most of the time she is already fed.

Primary and secondary caregiving mothers' level of education seems to have exposed them to recent research findings on the role of fathers in infants' development:

> *Mother:* When I was pregnant with Betty, we talked about it. But the other part of it is that I was doing my Post Doc in Valley Hospital. We were aware of the role of the father and Berry Brazelton [gave lectures] in which he spoke a lot about attachment and attachment with fathers. So, it was the topic of discussion. And when we were at Brown, Brazelton talked to Bob. So I guess just those kinds of issues were very much in our minds and we both talked about the roles that our fathers played in our development.
>
> *Father:* Or did not . . .
>
> *Mother:* Or did not for the most part, and Bob did not want to have that kind of relationship with his children. (*Secondary Mother, Primary Father*)

Mothers in both family types had adopted an ethic of sharing. However, the meaning of sharing caregiving duties varied for primary and secondary caregiving mothers. Involved in a rewarding career and having the same employment potential as their spouse, secondary caregiving mothers believed in an equal division of labor inside and outside the home. If their spouse was unemployed while they worked full-time, as was sometimes the case in the current study, then their spouse was to assume primary child-care responsibilities during the day:

> Since Eva was born, we decided we were going to share child-care responsibilities. We tried to figure a way to make it work. (*Secondary Mother*)

> The person who works all day in the evening watches the baby, and the other works around the house and makes dinner and does the laundry. (*Secondary Mother*)

Because of their level of education and openness to new psychological trends in infant care, primary caregiving fathers had rejected stereotypical beliefs concerning the role of fathers in child care:

> I understand that you do not want to share one day, but I get very bothered by men who seem to have the attitude that as soon as the kid needs anything, it's not their province. I do not think that is good. (*Primary Father*)

> I felt that I had to learn more about cooking and things like that. Then I spent five years as a teacher in nursery school, and I always felt that men should be more involved in raising kids and being teachers. (*Primary Father*)

Sharing often seemed to primary caregiving fathers the only fair arrangement since their spouse was also working:

> You know, we did not get married until we were in our thirties. I was taking care of myself already. I knew how to cook, and I did my laundry. So I just would not consider dumping all the work on her. (*Primary Father*)

> It seemed fair to me because of my flexible hours and Marcy has to work full-time. So why should I be the king? And it is good for the kids. (*Primary Father*)

> I think we should split the responsibilities, recognizing that if she has to wake up in the morning, I should do more so she can go to work. And,

you know, it has been very enjoyable. (*Primary Father*)

By contrast, the division of labor between primary caregiving mothers and their spouse was for mothers to assume the traditional role of child care during the day and for fathers to assume the role of breadwinner. Nevertheless, primary caregiving mothers and their spouse also believed that once home, fathers had to share and get involved in child care. A primary caregiving mother expressed her feelings and those of her friends:

> A lot of my girlfriends say that they are waiting at the door at 5:30 for their husbands to help them.

Secondary caregiving fathers also understood the need to help out:

> I believe it is important for a husband to help out. Julie would be frantic if I did not. And on weekends you know . . . . I know she is here all week with the kids and she needs a release. Sometimes I'll have the kids on Saturday. Because a happy wife is a happy family!

Employment and Attitude toward Work

Secondary caregiving mothers' employment potential differed from that of primary caregiving mothers. Secondary caregiving mothers held high-status occupations and were involved in rewarding careers. They were usually lawyers, psychologists, and architects, or self-employed. By contrast, primary caregiving mothers felt they had to abandon their career as teacher, day-care worker, or nurse to take care of their infants.

Primary and secondary caregiving fathers in this study had come to rethink the values that were important to them—achievement and professional success—versus fatherhood and family life:

> My father was very money oriented and always was at work. When I started my practice, I asked a few attorneys who had been through their careers if they had to change something what would they change. They all said they would have spent more time with their families, so I made a decision that I would spend more time with my family. (*Primary Father*)

> My father did not do very much in the house because he was always working, but I really love my child and I love my wife, and I know that things have to be done in the house also. I try to pick up the slack. Merryl points out things to me that I should do [he giggles]. (*Secondary Father*)

Although they were professionals, primary caregiving fathers were not overly career oriented. Child care was a totally different type of adventure they wanted to experience:

> I was not particularly thrilled with my boss at the time. Although I was happy to be working, I was not happy with the employer, and I always wanted to try it [to be a primary caregiver]. (*Primary Father*)

> It was important for both of us to be with him. We wanted to see him grow. I like not being at work full-time. It just is so much fun to do things with him. (*Primary Father*)

Nevertheless, many primary caregiving fathers did not want to stop altogether working outside the home but rather to strike a balance between staying at home and work. One primary caregiving father explained:

> *Father:* If we had more money, we would be home more.

> *Interviewer:* You would stop working?

> *Father:* Maybe for a while, but then I think I would want to get out of the house.

The flexibility of working hours was another important factor determining child-care arrangements. Whether professionals, students, professors, or self-employed, primary caregiving fathers enjoyed a flexible schedule, which allowed them to work around the hours they were taking care of their infants:

> I can arrange my schedule so that I can stay at home either two or three days. It is mostly economic. But largely also it is nice to have around her a parent as much as possible. (*Primary Father*)

> I knew that my schedule—because I taught—will provide some type of flexibility to stay at home. And we thought that if we can economically swing it, we would do it this way. (*Primary Father*)

> When we moved to Albany, instead of looking for a job that would demand fifty hours a week, I tried to establish a position that left the control of the position in my hands rather than in the employer's hands. So it depends on how busy I want to be with it. (*Primary Father*)

By contrast, some secondary caregiving fathers did not have too much leeway in scheduling their work hours. Some of them expressed regret at working forty hours a week:

> I work forty hours a week, and I see the kids on weekends. I would not mind spending more time with them though. (*Secondary Father*)

Family Financial Situation

The family's financial situation was also taken into account when deciding the type of child-care arrangement to be adopted. Most couples had come to the decision that the spouse who could earn the greatest salary and who had the greatest employment potential would be the one to work outside the home. In traditional families, secondary caregiving fathers generally were highly paid professionals, whereas primary caregiving mothers were not.

Some secondary caregiving fathers argued that their spouse's salary was so low that it would barely pay for alternative child care:

> But we found out that her income was just paying child care, so she decided to stay home. Financially we could swing it, when Mary tried a part-time job from 8:30 to 11:30 in the morning and it was too frustrating emotionally.

Some primary caregiving mothers also acknowledged that they could not trade places with their spouse, despite their spouse's willingness to do so, because they could not earn the same kind of money:

> *Interviewer:* How about switching roles?
>
> *Secondary Father:* It is okay with me!
>
> *Primary Mother:* With my salary we could not make it.

By contrast, in nontraditional families, secondary caregiving mothers generally held high-status professions and had the same employment potential as primary caregiving fathers. They could share working outside the home more equally:

Each of us works two days and a half at the state, so we also share in caregiving half and half. On Wednesday morning I pick my wife up at 12:45 and we make the switch. The only exception is that Melinda uses a babysitter the days she watches him because she does water coloring and it gives her the time to paint. (*Primary Father*)

Having only one of the partners working meant, in some cases, not being able to afford many commodities that two salaries could afford. Parents in both groups were, however, ready to sustain a financial loss and sometimes economic hardship in order to take care of their infants:

If we were both working, we would be able to afford a house, and maybe in that case we would have somebody that would come to clean. (*Secondary Mother*)

I feel torn because on the one hand I really would like to do something. I feel frustrated that I cannot earn any money. (*Primary Mother*)

We take a serious cut by me staying home. I am totally stressed and frantic over money, but I am not frantic over my choice to stay here. I really do not want to go back to work. Someone will just have to cut me off with this and that and limit everything, and we go through this all the time. (*Primary Mother*)

Primary caregiving fathers, nevertheless, argued that as long as they could get by with one salary, they would continue with their present child-care arrangement:

And Beth did her analysis of the budget [he laughs]. So I would not have tried it if it was breaking us financially. So, since it seemed plausible financially to do it and it was something I wanted to do, I did it. (*Primary Father*)

As long as we could swing it, I wanted to try it for at least a year. (*Primary Father*)

Very few primary and secondary caregiving mothers argued that they could afford taking a loss of a salary:

I wanted to be the primary caretaker for my children. I feel privileged that we can afford to do that. (*Primary Mother*)

Some people cannot afford giving up one of their salaries—but we could. (*Secondary Mother*)

Satisfaction with the Caregiving Role Assumed

Satisfaction with the present arrangement was also an incentive to keep it. Primary caregiving mothers enjoyed playing the traditional role of mothers. They loved to be mothers and to take care of their children:

My life has obviously changed. I feel that my life is enriched from my children. I always wanted to be a mother. I really love my family. I feel it is a positive change, although sometimes I am out of patience.

When asked whether they would like another kind of child-care arrangement or whether they wanted to go back to work, primary caregiving mothers in general answered, "No, I love to stay home!"

Primary caregiving mothers also shared with the interviewer the satisfaction that secondary caregiving fathers derived from sharing caregiving duties:

The part that I did not say is that he really wants to. He needs and wants to do things for Michael, and whenever they spent time together Michael plays with him. He is happy and playful, and when he puts his arms around him, he says that it makes him happier than anything.

Only two primary caregiving mothers complained that their spouse was not sufficiently committed to child rearing:

I would like him to have more of an active role . . . to know what has to be done and not to ask, "What do I have to do now?" (*Primary Mother*)

I wish that he would just know what is to be done and to be involved in it emotionally. To think what are the activities we are going to do today. Just to be involved in caregiving the way that I am involved in it. To love your kids, if you know what I mean. (*Secondary Mother*)

Others complained that their spouse worked too much outside the house and therefore could not help as much as they otherwise would have had they been more often at home:

> Bob works very hard. I think he puts a 100% effort when he is around. I would like him to have a more regular schedule so that we could have a regular night time together. (*Primary Mother*)

Past research has reported the satisfaction that primary caregiving fathers derived from greater involvement with their children and the consequent changes in their relationship (Gronseth, 1975; Russel, 1983). However, these fathers were taking care of toddlers and school-age children and rarely of infants. Thus, the child-care responsibilities assumed were less demanding than those assumed by fathers taking care of infants. Nevertheless, this difference did not prevent the primary caregiving fathers participating in the current study from reporting the same joy of watching their infants grow:

> Work is very task oriented, while what I do with him is open and free and flows in all different ways of looking at the world. (*Primary Father*)

> Playing with him and watching him do something for the first time and that kind of thing is a real treat. (*Primary Father*)

> It is really rewarding and challenging to see him grow. The feeling of nurturing is wonderful. His joy of learning about the world is fun to watch. (*Primary Father*)

> He is such an enrichment to our lives. He is so cute and easy to have around. He is wonderful! (*Primary Father*)

> It is maybe wishful thinking, but I believe that I have established with him a relationship that will last for a lifetime. (*Primary Father*)

Comparing past and present child-care arrangements, a primary caregiving father reported how much closer he had become to his infant:

> I feel I missed something with Diane (older child). She is close to her mother, and she is never like that with me. Melanie (infant) will stick to me later, while Diane will stick to her mother.

Expressing themselves in a "we" voice, several secondary caregiving mothers also expressed their satisfaction by stating that even if they had more money to hire a nanny, they would prefer the present arrangement:

> If we had money . . . like we have somebody who comes and cleans the house every other week, we probably would have her come and clean the house more often. But I do not think I would hire somebody to watch the girls.

Reactions of Others

The reaction of others could have prevented fathers from adopting a child-care arrangement so different from the traditional one. Primary caregiving fathers who went to play groups with their infant sometimes reported that they felt strange, at first, to be the only males in all women play groups. They had to get used to topics of conversation to which they had previously never paid attention to:

> Instead of stocks and bonds and where to invest, they talked about toilet training, diaper rashes, or feeding the baby.

Some women in malls felt sorry for these fathers and their infant, as if their spouse had abandoned them. They were treated as helpless:

> They always climb all over me and offer to put on the baby's snowsuit. (*Primary Father*)

Lack of understanding, negative comments, and sarcasm were at times the reactions of primary caregiving mothers. After primary caregiving fathers answered to their question "What is your profession?" with "I take care of my kid," these mothers kept on asking, "But what do you do?"—as if it is not enough for males to be full-time fathers as it is for females to be full-time mothers.

Other primary caregiving mothers called primary caregiving fathers "full-time Mr. Dad." A secondary caregiving mother noted the sarcasm of some of her colleagues:

> People always say to me, 'You better watch it. He may like it at home!'

However, the majority of nontraditional parents reported support in their new role from their surrounding community:

People are very receptive. It depends on the attitude you project. If you project an attitude of helplessness, then people will pick up on that. I never felt like that and people react to that. (*Primary Father*)

Reporting the comments of her colleagues at work, a secondary caregiving mother stated:

People tell me that it is easy for me, because I know that he is staying home with Andrew. They tell me that if he was in day care, I would not feel so comfortable.

Primary caregiving fathers also reported the support of their bosses:

My office gave me a leave without pay. I was very lucky that my director was so supportive about it because not too many people do it. (*Primary Father*)

So I made a pitch in the office and I told them that I wanted to do it, and they said OK. (*Primary Father*)

Where I work people are very understanding. It would have been very different if we had stayed in Nebraska. Even taking a six-week paternity leave, which is allowed by law, would have been looked down upon in the corporation I worked for in Nebraska. The situation would have been more problematic in terms of how to negotiate things. (*Primary Father*)

So despite some negative reactions of others, the support of their bosses and others contributed to primary caregiving fathers' satisfaction with the present caregiving arrangements.

PATTERNS OF SHARING IN CAREGIVING

Examination of self-report data concerning the way the caregiving tasks of bathing the baby, feeding, diapering, comforting, and putting the baby to sleep were actually shared between spouses reveals important differences between the sharing pattern of nontraditional and traditional families. Tables 4.2–4.6 show how these tasks were shared in both family types.

Table 4.2
Parent Bathing Baby When Both Parents Home:
Frequency Count

	Nontrad Families		Trad Families	
	n	Pct	n	Pct
Mostly Mother	0	0%	6	43%
Mostly Father	5	36%	1	7%
Both Share	9	64%	7	50%
	14	100%	14	100%

Note: Nontrad = Nontraditional; Trad = Traditional.

Table 4.3
Parent Feeding Baby When Both Parents Home:
Frequency Count

	Nontrad Families		Trad Families	
	n	Pct	n	Pct
Mostly Mother	1	7%	7	50%
Mostly Father	3	21%	0	0%
Both Share	10	71%	7	50%
	14	99%*	14	100%

Notes: Nontrad = Nontraditional; Trad = Traditional. *Due to rounding error, some percentages do not sum to 100%.

Table 4.4
Parent Diapering Baby When Both Parents Home:
Frequency Count

	Nontrad Families		Trad Families	
	n	Pct	n	Pct
Mostly Mother	0	0%	7	50%
Mostly Father	2	14%	0	0%
Both Share	12	86%	7	50%
	14	100%	14	100%

Note: Nontrad = Nontraditional; Trad = Traditional.

Table 4.5
Parent Comforting Baby When Both Parents Home:
Frequency Count

	Nontrad Families		Trad Families	
	n	Pct	n	Pct
Mostly Mother	0	0%	7	50%
Mostly Father	1	7%	0	0%
Both Share	13	93%	7	50%
	14	100%	14	100%

Note: Nontrad = Nontraditional; Trad = Traditional.

Table 4.6
Parent Putting Baby to Sleep When Both Parents Home:
Frequency Count

	Nontrad Families		Trad Families	
	n	Pct	n	Pct
Mostly Mother	1	7%	11	79%
Mostly Father	2	14%	1	7%
Both Share	11	79%	2	14%
	14	100%	14	100%

Note: Nontrad = Nontraditional; Trad = Traditional.

When both parents were at home during the week in the evening or on weekends, 64 to 93 percent of primary caregiving fathers, as opposed to up to 50 percent of secondary caregiving fathers, reported sharing equally with their spouse the tasks of bathing, feeding, diapering, comforting, and putting the baby to sleep. Another difference noted was that whenever caregiving duties were not shared, they were assumed by primary caregiving fathers in nontraditional families and by primary caregiving mothers in traditional families.

Whether primary or secondary caregivers, fathers proved themselves to be very competent at caregiving. They were aware of their infants' needs and of the timing of each caregiving task. In the words of primary caregiving fathers, they were "pretty much interchangeable" with mothers.

I fed her, changed her diapers, gave her a bottle, played with her, then I put her to bed. (*Primary Father*)

He eats breakfast, then we play around the house, then he takes a nap between 10 A.M. and 11 A.M. for one hour, then he gets up and he takes a bottle for fifteen minutes. Then we go out to a park. (*Primary Father*)

The two girls were sleeping and Marcy had left so I got them up, fed them, gave them both a bath, dried and combed Melinda's hair. You know, the whole thing! (*Primary Father*)

A secondary caregiving father also described the way he took care of his baby girl:

Father: When I come back before dinner, I try to help feed her dinner. Then she hangs out for an hour. I play with her.

Interviewer: Then you put her to bed?

Father: Then we give her a bath.

Interviewer: Together?

Father: Yes, together. It's a lot of fun actually!

Primary caregiving mothers also reported how helpful secondary caregiving fathers were once they came back from work:

Mother: He changes diapers and all that stuff.

Interviewer: Does she accept to be put to bed by you?

Mother: Yes, and at bed time also. He rocks her in the rocking chair and then he puts her to bed.

Father: And then I sing to her with my melodious voice! (*Primary Mother, Secondary Father*)

The few primary caregiving mothers who had prevented their spouse from sharing expressed regret for not having allowed divergence in the manner of diapering or feeding the baby. They had never been satisfied with the way their spouse put on the diapers or the mess they made while feeding the baby. After a while, their spouse stopped assuming caregiving duties.

I think I have unfortunately been too critical. He is not overzealous, but he is very willing to change diapers. Sometimes, I may have been too critical about what George has done and maybe I have pulled him away from doing it. And if this is so, I will never forgive myself, because when you come down on somebody, they never want to do it again. (*Primary Mother*)

Another primary caregiving mother claimed that her infant would not let his father attend to his needs:

A big part of it is that he is willing to do it, but Billy does not let him. Like if he takes him to the room and changes his diapers, he starts

screaming and carrying on, and then I have to go in and calm him down.
Even if he changes his diaper, I have to stand there just that he stays still!

Still other primary caregiving mothers thought that it was impossible to
share with their spouse certain tasks such as putting the baby to sleep. They
believed they had to nurse their babies to sleep. By contrast, secondary
caregiving mothers nursed their babies before they went to bed and left the
baby's room to allow their spouse to put the baby to sleep. A primary
caregiving father thus explains:

If she is not around or if she walks out of the room, I can put her to
sleep. But if we are both in the room, Amanda will want to nurse.

The pattern for getting up at night was found to be quite different. In
nontraditional and traditional families alike, getting up at night remained
most of the time mothers' task (Table 4.7). While some primary caregiving
fathers (29%) shared this task equally with their spouse, very few fathers,
whether primary (14%) or secondary (14%) caregivers, assumed this task
most of the time.

Table 4.7
Parent Getting up at Night: Frequency Count

	Nontrad Families		Trad Families	
	n	Pct	n	Pct
Mostly Mother	6	43%	8	58%
Father Shares Weekends	0	0%	2	14%
Mostly Father	2	14%	2	14%
Take Turns	4	29%	0	0%
Never Get Up at Night	2	14%	2	14%
	14	100%	14	100%

Note: Nontrad = Nontraditional; Trad = Traditional.

The few fathers who uniquely assumed the task of waking up at night explained that they did so to gain sleeping time. Whenever infants saw their father they went right back to sleep, whereas their mother's appearance was an invitation to stay up:

> Sometimes Melanie [baby] gets up in the middle of the night because she has a bad dream or something. Marc [father] always gets up at night. If I get up, she would want to nurse. When I traveled to California last summer, it was horrible because she got up a lot and she would want to nurse. (*Primary Mother*)

> If I go in, he won't go back to sleep. Paul goes in and tells him to go back to sleep and he goes back. (*Primary Mother*)

HOUSEHOLD CHORES AND PLAY

Despite numerous caregiving tasks to be assumed, primary caregiving fathers' major occupation remains playing with their infant.

> On Monday we have a play group we go to, and then in the afternoon he likes to be outside a great deal. He likes to kick the ball, so we play with the ball. We play in the sand box, or we visit some neighbor who is three years old that he chases. That's basically it. On Tuesday, we go to another play group at the community center in the morning. He likes to drive or play in the house. On Wednesday, it is complicated because I have to play with him and also get ready for work. (*Primary Father*)

> We read a lot and we just play. Practice rolling balls, blocks, we go for walks. When the weather is warmer we will probably go for hikes and stuff like that. And she does errands with me. We go to the library, and if I have an emergency, she'll come with me either to court or to the library where I am doing some research. (*Primary Father*)

Primary caregiving fathers could also stay at home and just relax with their infants:

> Some days we are lucky—we get to stay home. Some days we stay in bed and fool around. Tomorrow is one of these days!

Household chores such as cooking and cleaning were performed as a routine, about which primary caregiving fathers were not overly concerned. In the words of a primary caregiving father:

> What I do is mainly what is repetitious. But if it's something like how to treat a certain stain in laundry, I would put everything together in the washing machine, put in on hot hot, and run everything. And it's the same thing with cleaning. I either do not care or do not see or choose not to see something that bothers me. If I did get involved in it, I probably would get so obsessed that I would not be able to get past a corner. So, Mary [wife] does it.

Moreover, household chores certainly did not come before playing:

> We go out to a park and play or we just go out for a walk or play around the house. Then we eat lunch and around one o'clock he takes a nap and wakes up around 4 P.M. Then he drinks a bottle and we play, and then I start dinner and he plays by himself. (*Primary Father*)

By contrast, primary caregiving mothers seemed to be obsessed with cleaning the house and often felt they had no time for play. They perceived motherhood to be a job and so was cleaning and cooking. They seemed to have missed the element of fun that primary caregiving fathers had while they were playing with their infants. In the words of a secondary caregiving mother:

> He has more patience with him—I clean. When I am with him, I have him, but I am not playing with him, he devotes much more his time to Alan.

For most primary and secondary caregiving mothers, playing with their infants for ten minutes, as they were instructed to do in the current study, "seemed awfully long." Some of them also confessed that they had really never played with their infants for such an extended period of time:

> The honest truth is that I do not play too much with him. I just take all the toys out, and he entertains himself. (*Primary Mother*)

> I do not often get down on the floor and play with her. I interact with her while doing something else. (*Secondary Mother*)

Primary caregiving mothers also indicated that they usually interacted with their infant while busy doing something else:

> I do not play with her all that much. She usually does what I do. I am
> cleaning house. I am doing things, and she plays around me. You know
> you cannot do that [play] when you stay at home.

CONCLUSION

In conclusion, several factors combine to explain why nontraditional and traditional parents alike had adopted the child-care arrangement in which one of the parents stayed at home with the infant. These include parents' attitudes toward child care and day care, their educational background, employment potential and working schedule, as well as their beliefs about the roles men and women play in child care.

Interview data revealed that nontraditional families, in which fathers were the primary caregivers, were more egalitarian than the reference group of traditional families. Most primary caregiving fathers, but only half of the secondary caregiving fathers, shared equally caregiving duties with their spouse when they were at home on weekdays, in the evenings, and on weekends. Also, whenever these duties were not shared, they were generally assumed by primary caregiving fathers in nontraditional families, whereas in the reference group of traditional families they were assumed by primary caregiving mothers.

Despite the noted differences, the interview data indicate that the conventional characterization of fathers reported in earlier studies (Kotelchuck, 1976; Newland, 1980; Russel, 1983) as working all day outside the home, never caregiving, and barely playing with their infant is no longer realistic. Whatever the caregiving role, once at home, most of the fathers in the sample did play with their infant and did assume several caregiving responsibilities such as bathing, feeding, diaper changing, comforting, and putting the baby to sleep. In fact, it was hard if not impossible to find secondary caregiving fathers who were not involved in caregiving. Some primary caregiving mothers complained that their spouse was not sufficiently committed to child rearing, while others complained that their spouse returned too late from work and thus could not help as much as he otherwise would have had he been home earlier. Yet, no primary caregiving mother complained that her spouse refused to change diapers or never played with their infant.

Interview data also indicate that the amount of caregiving duties assumed was based on the caregiving role rather than on the gender of the caregiver. Whether male or female, the spouse who had the greater employment potential or a highly paid occupation worked full-time outside the home and assumed secondary caregiving duties. The other spouse (father or mother) assumed primary caregiving duties. And even though secondary caregiving spouses were found to be sharing once at home, primary caregivers (fathers and mothers) continued to assume the greatest load of caregiving responsibilities. The exception concerns the task of getting up at night, for which the gender of the caregiver rather than the caregiving role assumed greater influence. It was predominantly mothers' job to wake up at night, possibly because of the need to nurse the baby.

Primary caregiving fathers and mothers spent in absolute terms more time with their infants than did secondary caregiving fathers and mothers who came back from work at 6 P.M. However, the amount of time dedicated to play as well as the attitude toward play were related to the gender of the caregiver rather than to the caregiving role assumed. Whether primary or secondary caregivers, fathers were more relaxed and more fully involved in play with their infants than were mothers. Primary and secondary caregiving mothers rarely stopped performing other chores to play with their infant. They usually interacted with their infant while busy cooking or cleaning.

OBSERVATIONAL DATA

To test the research questions, it was necessary to complement the data provided in the parental interviews with more controlled data. Thus, home observations of parent-interaction were conducted and then analyzed into affiliative and attachment behaviors that parents and infants displayed toward each other. The goal was to investigate the unique and interactive effects of the gender of the caregiver and the primacy of the caregiver role on caregivers' and infants' behaviors.

Data analysis was carried out on the affiliative and attachment behaviors of the four categories of caregivers produced by the various possible combinations of the gender of the caregiver and primacy of the caregiver role: primary caregiving fathers, secondary caregiving mothers, secondary caregiving fathers, and primary caregiving mothers. The same type of analysis was also performed on the affiliative and attachment behaviors infants exhibited under nonstressful and stressful conditions toward the four categories of caregivers.

The independent and dependent measures of this study are recapitulated here. The independent measures were:

1. Gender of the caregiver: male or female.

2. Primacy of the caregiver's role: primary or secondary.

Another possible independent measure—gender of the infant—was eliminated from the analysis because the dichotomy would have made the number of subjects in each subsample too small to allow for statistical manipulation. All dependent measures were coded in frequency counts of twenty-second time segments in which the criterion behavior was demonstrated.

The dependent measures of episodes 1 and 2 were:

1. Parents' affiliative behavior analyzed into: holding, looking, talking, playing with books, playing conventional games, playing rough-and-tumble.

2. Parents' attachment behavior analyzed into: caregiving behaviors and displaying affection.

3. Infants' affiliative behavior analyzed into: child resisting parent's activity, child initiating an activity, child involving parent in an activity, playing together with parent, playing alone, looking, smiling/laughing, and vocalizing.

4. Infants' attachment behavior analyzed into: displaying affection, moving away, exploring objects, approaching, proximity maintaining, and clinging.

The dependent measures of episode 3 were:

1. Infants' attachment behavior under stress analyzed into: proximity maintaining and seeking, social referencing (looking), turning body toward the parent, physical contact or physically resisting mother or father.

2. Infants' preferential attachment under stress was determined by the greatest number of attachment behaviors directed toward one of the parents who were both present during all of episode 3.

STATISTICAL ANALYSIS

To analyze the data, a repeated measures (gender of the caregiver X primacy' of the caregiver role[1]) analysis of variance (ANOVA) was computed by using as dependent variables the behaviors coded in episodes 1 through 3. The effect of each independent variable on the dependent measures was analyzed separately and in interaction. The purpose was to find out what were the main and interactive effects of the gender of the caregiver and the primacy of the caregiver role on the affiliative and attachment behaviors of parents and infants toward each other. Descriptive statistics using mean frequencies, standard deviations, and subsequent t tests have been used to conduct more-focused comparisons concerning the affiliative and attachment behaviors of the caregivers and their infants. The goal was to pinpoint significant gender, role, or interaction differences that might have been left unnoticed during the analysis of variance.

As noted in chapter 3, most parents' and infants' affiliative and attachment behaviors were found to correlate significantly ($p<.05$) from one session to the other. For that reason it was decided for simplicity and clarity of statistical analysis to combine the mean frequencies obtained for each behavior coded in session 1 and session 2 into average mean frequencies.

ANALYSIS OF CAREGIVERS' AFFILIATIVE AND ATTACHMENT BEHAVIORS

A repeated measures multivariate analysis of variance was conducted in order to answer the first research question concerning the unique and interactive effects of the independent variables—parent gender (male, female) and caregiving role (primary, secondary)—on parents' behavior toward their infant. Each dependent measure of parents' affiliative and attachment behavior, coded in this study from 0 to 30 time segments, was analyzed separately and in interaction (Table 4.8).

Gender Effect on Caregivers' Affiliative Behavior

As indicated in Table 4.8, a caregiver gender effect was observed on the affiliative behavior rough-and-tumble play ($F[1,52] = 13.54$, $p<.001$) and on the attachment behavior displays affection ($F[1,52] = 7.91$, $p<.007$). No main caregiver gender effect was observed on the remaining affiliative behaviors that the parents displayed toward their infant—holds, looks, talks, and plays with books or conventional games—and on the attachment behavior of caregiving.

To clarify the nature of significant gender effect observed during the analysis of variance, comparisons were performed concerning the behaviors of caregivers of opposite gender who assumed the same caregiving role. In this manner, primary caregiving fathers were compared to primary caregiving mothers (Table 4.9), and secondary caregiving fathers were compared to secondary caregiving mothers (Table 4.10) in the mean frequencies with which they engaged in rough-and-tumble play and displayed affection. (See Appendix F, Table F.1, for the mean frequencies of all parents' affiliative and attachment behaviors coded in this study.)

Table 4.8
Influence of Caregiver Gender and Caregiving Role on Caregivers'
Behaviors: ANOVA

	Gender		Role		Gender X Role	
Affiliative Behavior	F(1,52)	Sig	F(1,52)	Sig	F(1,52)	Sig
Holds	–	–	–	–	–	–
Looks at	–	–	–	–	–	–
Talks to Child	–	–	–	–	–	–
Plays with Books	–	–	–	–	–	–
Games Conventional	–	–	–	–	–	–
Rough and Tumble	13.54	.001	–	–	–	–
Attachment Behavior						
Caregives	–	–	2.68	.10	–	–
Displays Affection	7.91	.007	15.32	.0001	4.62	.036

Note: All F tests whose significance level exceeded $p > .10$ are indicated by dashes (–).

Table 4.9
Gender Differences in Primary Caregivers' Behaviors

	Prim	Fa	Prim	Mo		
	n = 14		n = 14			
Affiliative Behavior	Mean	SD	Mean	SD	t(26)	Prob
Rough and Tumble	1.36	1.18	.36	.72	2.70	.01
Attachment Behavior						
Displays Affection	2.75	1.89	1.14	.99	2.82	.009

Notes: Prim Fa = Primary Caregiving Fathers; Prim Mo = Primary Caregiving
Mothers. Parents' behavior coding ranged from 0 to 30 time segments.

Table 4.10
Gender Differences in Secondary Caregivers' Behaviors

	Second Fa		Second Mo			
	n = 14		n = 14			
Affiliative Behavior	Mean	SD	Mean	SD	t(26)	Prob
Rough and Tumble	2.11	2.68	.14	.31	2.73	.01
Attachment Behavior						
Displays Affection	.79	.96	.57	.65	.70	–

Notes: Second Fa = Secondary Caregiving Fathers; Second Mo = Secondary
Caregiving Mothers. Parents' behavior coding ranged from 0 to 30 time segments.
All significance levels exceeding $p > .10$ are indicated by dashes (–).

As indicated in Tables 4.9 and 4.10, rough-and-tumble play distinguished
both categories of fathers from both categories of mothers. Whether primary
or secondary caregivers, fathers engaged in more ($p < .01$) rough-and-tumble
play than did mothers. Primary caregiving fathers were also found to
display more ($p < .01$) affection than did primary caregiving mothers. By
contrast, secondary caregiving fathers and mothers did not significantly
($p > .10$) differ in the frequency with which they displayed affection toward
their infants.

The data thus show that regardless of the caregiving role assumed
(primary or secondary), fathers engaged in more rough-and-tumble play with
their infant than did mothers. However, since by comparison to secondary
caregiving fathers, only primary caregiving fathers were found to display
more affection toward their infant than did primary caregiving mothers, the
frequency with which fathers displayed affection was not uniquely
influenced by the gender of the caregiver.

Effect of Role on Caregivers' Affiliative and Attachment Behaviors

Examination of the analysis of variance performed in Table 4.8 indicates
no main role effect on any of the parents' affiliative behaviors—holds,
looks, talks, plays with books or conventional games, and rough-and-tumble
play—examined separately. By contrast, main role effects were observed on
the parents' attachment behaviors of display of affection ($F[1,52] = 15.32$,
$p < .0001$), and caregiving ($F[1,52] = 2.68$, $p < .10$).

To clarify the nature of significant role effects observed during the analysis of variance, comparisons of the attachment behaviors of caregivers of the same gender but assuming different roles were performed using mean frequencies, standard deviations, and subsequent t tests. In this manner, primary caregiving fathers were compared to secondary caregiving fathers (Table 4.11) and primary caregiving mothers to secondary caregiving mothers (Table 4.12) on the frequency with which they displayed affection toward their infant and engaged in caregiving behaviors.

Table 4.11
Caregiving Role Differences in Fathers' Attachment Behaviors

| | Prim Fa | | Second Fa | | | |
| | n = 14 | | n = 14 | | | |
Attachment Behavior	Mean	SD	Mean	SD	t(26)	Prob
Caregives	2.11	2.70	.64	.94	8.07	.001
Displays Affection	2.75	1.89	.79	.96	3.47	.003

Notes: Prim Fa = Primary Caregiving Fathers; Second Fa = Secondary Caregiving Fathers.   Parents' behavior coding ranged from 0 to 30 time segments.

Table 4.12
Caregiving Role Differences in Mothers' Attachment Behaviors

| | Prim Mo | | Second Mo | | | |
| | n = 14 | | n = 14 | | | |
Attachment Behavior	Mean	SD	Mean	SD	t(26)	Prob
Caregives	1.46	2.58	1.17	1.09	.38	–
Displays Affection	1.14	.99	.57	.65	1.81	.08

Notes: Prim Mo = Primary Caregiving Mothers; Second Mo = Secondary Caregiving Mothers.   Parents' behavior coding ranged from 0 to 30 time segments. All significance levels exceeding p>.10 are indicated by dashes (–).

As indicated in Table 4.11, primary caregiving fathers displayed more ($p<.003$) affection and engaged in more ($p<.001$) caregiving behaviors than did secondary caregiving fathers. By contrast (Table 4.12), although primary caregiving mothers displayed slightly ($p<.08$) more affection toward their infant than did secondary caregiving mothers, both categories of mothers were quite similar ($p>.10$) in the frequency with which they engaged in caregiving behaviors.

In summary, data show no caregiver role effect on all caregivers' affiliative behavior. Whatever caregiving role assumed, parents were similar in the frequency with which they held, looked, talked, played games, and rough-and-tumbled. By contrast, parents' attachment behaviors were influenced by the caregiving role they assumed. Differences in caregiving and displaying affection were much more pronounced between primary and secondary caregiving fathers than between primary and secondary caregiving mothers.

Interaction Effects on Caregivers' Affiliative and Attachment Behaviors

Examination of the analysis of variance performed on parents' affiliative and attachment behavior (Table 4.8) indicated no gender X role interaction effect on any one of the dependent measures of affiliation: holds, looks, talks, plays games or plays rough-and-tumble. By contrast, a gender X role interaction effect was observed on the attachment behavior of display of affection ($F[1,52] = 4.62$, $p<.036$).

Families in the study were comprised of one father and one mother, one of whom was the primary and the other the secondary caregiver. "Nontraditional families" were those in which the father was the primary caregiver; "traditional families" were those in which the mother was the primary caregiver. It was meaningful to explore in more detail the sources of gender X role interaction effect within traditional and nontraditional families. Table 4.13 allows this by showing the mean frequencies, standard deviations, and t tests indicating significant differences between the affiliative and attachment behaviors of primary caregiving fathers and secondary caregiving mothers within nontraditional families. Table 4.14 presents the data showing a significant difference between the behaviors of secondary caregiving fathers and primary caregiving mothers within traditional families.

Table 4.13
Parents' Behavior Differences within Nontraditional Families

	Prim Fa n = 14		Second Mo n = 14			
	Mean	SD	Mean	SD	t(26)	Prob
Affiliative Behavior						
Rough and Tumble	1.36	1.18	.14	.31	3.72	.002
Attachment Behavior						
Displays Affection	2.75	1.89	.57	.65	4.08	.001

Notes: Prim Fa = Primary Caregiving Fathers; Second Mo = Secondary Caregiving Mothers. Parents' behavior coding ranged from 0 to 30 time segments.

Table 4.14
Parents' Behavior Differences within Traditional Families

	Second Fa n = 14		Prim Mo n = 14			
	Mean	SD	Mean	SD	t(26)	Prob
Affiliative Behavior						
Rough and Tumble	2.11	2.68	.36	.72	2.36	.02
Attachment Behavior						
Displays Affection	.79	.96	1.14	.99	-.97	–

Notes: Second Fa = Secondary Caregiving Fathers; Prim Mo = Primary Caregiving Mothers. Parents' behavior coding ranged from 0 to 30 time segments. All significance levels exceeding $p > .10$ are indicated by dashes (–).

As indicated in Tables 4.13 and 4.14, rough-and-tumble play was the only affiliative behavior significantly differentiating mothers from fathers within nontraditional and traditional families. The attachment behavior of displays affection differentiated ($p < .01$) fathers from mothers only within nontraditional families (Table 4.13). Within traditional families, fathers and mothers were similar ($p > .10$) in the frequency with which they displayed affection toward their infants (Table 4.14).

Summary and Conclusion: Caregiver Gender and Caregiving Role Effects on Parents' Behaviors

No main caregiver gender, caregiving role, or gender X role interaction effect was observed on most parents' affiliative behaviors coded in this study. These findings suggest that primary caregiving fathers were similar to secondary caregiving mothers and fathers and to primary caregiving mothers in the frequency with which they held, looked, talked, and played with books or conventional games with their infant. The exception concerns rough-and-tumble play, for which a main gender effect was observed. Whether primary or secondary caregivers, fathers engaged in more rough-and-tumble play than did mothers.

Analysis of variance also indicated main gender, role, and interaction effects on the parents' attachment behavior of display of affection. More-focused comparisons show that the caregiving role ($r = .44$) explained a greater proportion of the variance than gender of the caregiver ($r = .33$) on this measure. The primacy of the caregiving role was also found to influence the caregiving behavior of fathers but not that of mothers. Primary caregiving fathers performed more caregiving duties than secondary caregiving fathers did, whereas primary and secondary caregiving mothers performed the same amount of caregiving duties. These findings are supported by the interview data, which indicate that secondary caregiving mothers usually shared caregiving duties equally with their spouse once at home. Thus, their caregiving behavior did not significantly differ from that of primary caregiving mothers. By contrast, the caregiving behavior of secondary caregiving fathers did differ from that of primary caregiving fathers, because only up to 50 percent of secondary caregiving fathers reported sharing caregiving duties equally with their spouse once they came back from work.

These findings also suggest that the primacy of the caregiver role has a more pronounced effect than the gender of the caregiver on caregivers' attachment behaviors toward their infant. Primary caregiving fathers were similar to primary and secondary caregiving mothers in the amount of caregiving tasks they performed. Primary caregiving fathers were also found to be the most affectionate category of caregivers. Finally, even though primary caregiving fathers engaged in more attachment behaviors than secondary caregiving fathers, they did not abandon the rough-and-tumble play style characteristic of secondary caregiving father-infant interaction. Fathers' play style thus remained unaffected by the caregiving role assumed and the resultant change in daily child-care involvement.

ANALYSIS OF INFANTS' AFFILIATIVE AND ATTACHMENT BEHAVIORS IN A NONSTRESSFUL SITUATION

An analysis of variance was also conducted to answer the second research question concerning the unique and interactive effects of the gender of the caregiver and the primacy of caregiving role on infants' affiliative and attachment behavior. These measures, obtained while infants interacted with one parent at a time in a nonstressful situation, were analyzed separately and in interaction (Table 4.15).

Table 4.15
Influence of Caregiver Gender and Role on Infants' Behaviors in a Nonstressful Situation: ANOVA

Affiliative Behavior	Gender F(1,52)	Sig	Role F(1,52)	Sig	Gender X Role F(1,52)	Role Sig
Resists Parent	–	–	–	–	–	–
Initiates Activity	–	–	–	–	12.34	.001
Involves Parent	–	–	4.31	.04	17.05	.0001
Plays Together	–	–	–	–	–	–
Plays Alone	–	–	–	–	–	–
Looks at Parent	–	–	–	–	–	–
Smiles or Laughs	–	–	–	–	–	–
Vocalizes	–	–	–	–	–	–
Attachment Behavior						
Displays Affection	–	–	9.86	.003	–	–
Moves Away	–	–	–	–	7.27	.009
Explores Objects	–	–	–	–	3.84	.055
Approaches	–	–	–	–	–	–
In Proximity	–	–	–	–	–	–
Clings or Climbs	–	–	–	–	4.45	.04

Note: All F tests whose significance level exceeded p>.10 are indicated by dashes (–).

Effect of Caregiver Gender on Infants' Affiliative and Attachment Behaviors in a Nonstressful Situation

As indicated in Table 4.15, no main caregiver gender effect was observed on any of the infants' affiliative behaviors—resisting parent's activity, initiating activity, infant involving parent in activity, playing with parent, playing alone, smiling/laughing, vocalizing, and looking—coded in this study (all p values >.10). Similarly, no main gender effect was observed on any of the infants' attachment behaviors—displays affection, moves away, explores, approaches, in proximity, and clings.

Some differences based on gender could, however, be observed once more-focused comparisons using t tests were performed on infants' behaviors toward caregivers of opposite gender who assumed the same caregiving role. Table 4.16 indicates significant differences in infants' behaviors toward fathers and mothers who assumed primary caregiving duties. Table 4.17 indicates significant differences in infants' behaviors in the presence of fathers and mothers who assumed secondary caregiving duties. (Mean frequencies for all infants' affiliative and attachment behaviors coded in this study may be found in Appendix F, Table F.2.) Table 4.16 shows that infants more often (p<.007) initiated an activity and more often (p<.002) involved in an activity fathers than mothers who assumed a primary caregiving role. Similarly, infants more often (p<.06) moved away from fathers than from mothers who assumed a primary caregiving role.

Table 4.16
Parent Gender Effects on Infants' Behaviors toward Primary Caregivers in a Nonstressful Situation

	Prim	Fa	Prim	Mo		
	n = 14		n = 14			
Affiliative Behavior	Mean	SD	Mean	SD	t(26)	Prob
Initiates Activity	8.54	3.34	5.11	2.82	2.94	.007
Involves Parent	9.89	4.06	5.43	2.14	3.64	.002
Attachment Behavior						
Moves Away	6.43	2.81	4.29	2.87	2.00	.06

Notes: Prim Fa = Primary Caregiving Fathers; Second Mo = Secondary Caregiving Mothers. Infants' behavior coding ranged from 0 to 30 time segments.

Table 4.17
**Parent Gender Effects on Infants' Behaviors toward Secondary
Caregivers in a Nonstressful Situation**

	Second Fa		Second Mo			
	n = 14		n = 14			
Affiliative Behavior	Mean	SD	Mean	SD	t(26)	Prob
Initiates Activity	5.07	2.08	6.68	2.31	-1.93	.07
Involves Parent	5.04	2.19	7.04	2.91	-2.06	.05
Attachment Behavior						
Moves Away	4.29	2.35	6.32	3.47	-1.82	.08

Notes: Second Fa = Secondary Caregiving Fathers; Second Mo = Secondary
Caregiving Mothers. Infants' behavior coding ranged from 0 to 30 time segments.

By contrast, as shown in Table 4.17, infants more often initiated an activity ($p<.07$), more often involved ($p<.05$), and slightly more often moved away ($p<.08$) when in the presence of secondary caregiving mothers than they did when in the presence of secondary caregiving fathers.

In summary, no gender effect was observed on most of the infants' affiliative and attachment behaviors toward their parents in a nonstressful situation. These findings indicate that the gender of the caregiver (father or mother) did not significantly affect the frequency with which infants resisted the parent's activity, played with the parent, played alone, smiled/laughed, vocalized, and looked at the parent, nor the frequency with which infants displayed affection, explored, approached, were in proximity of the parent, or clung to the parent in a nonstressful situation. Differences based on gender were, however, observed on infants initiating an activity, involving parent in activity, and moving away. Infants were found to exhibit these behaviors more often in the presence of fathers than in the presence of mothers who assumed primary caregiving duties. This finding suggests a greater degree of synchronous interaction between primary caregiving fathers and their infant. This finding is consistent with the interview data, which indicated that despite a similar amount of caregiving tasks to be assumed, primary caregiving fathers were more involved in their infant's play than were primary caregiving mothers. Primary caregiving mothers also noted that they usually interacted with their infants while busy performing other chores.

Effect of Caregiving Role on Infants' Affiliative and Attachment Behaviors

The analysis of variance performed in Table 4.15 indicates a significant role effect on the affiliative behavior of involving parent in an activity ($F[1,52] = 4.31$, $p<.04$) and on the attachment behavior of displays affection ($F[1,52] = 9.86$, $p<.003$).

In order to investigate the nature of significance of the caregiver role effect observed during the analysis of variance, more-focused comparisons were performed using mean frequencies, standard deviations, and subsequent t tests. These comparisons concerned significant differences in the affiliative and attachment behaviors of infants toward caregivers of the same gender who assumed different caregiving roles. Differences in the affiliative and attachment behavior of infants toward primary and secondary caregiving fathers appear in Table 4.18, while those toward primary and secondary caregiving mothers are presented in Table 4.19.

Table 4.18
Fathers' Caregiving Role Effects on Infants' Behaviors in a Nonstressful Situation

	Prim Fa		Second Fa			
	n = 14		n = 14			
Affiliative Behavior	Mean	SD	Mean	SD	t(26)	Prob
Initiates Activity	8.54	3.34	5.07	2.08	3.29	.003
Involves Parent	9.89	4.06	5.04	2.19	3.94	.001
Attachment Behavior						
Displays Affection	.36	.50	.04	.13	2.34	.03
Moves Away	6.43	2.81	4.29	2.35	2.19	.04

Notes: Prim Fa = Primary Caregiving Fathers; Second Fa = Secondary Caregiving Fathers. Infants' behavior coding ranged from 0 to 30 time segments.

As indicated in Table 4.18, infants more often involved ($\underline{p}$<.001) and more often initiated an activity ($\underline{p}$<.003) when in the presence of primary caregiving fathers than they did when in the presence of secondary caregiving fathers. Infants also displayed significantly ($\underline{p}$<.03) more affection toward primary caregiving fathers than they did toward secondary caregiving fathers. Similarly, infants more frequently ($\underline{p}$<.04) moved away from primary caregiving fathers than they did from secondary caregiving fathers.

By contrast, as shown in Table 4.19, infants did not differ significantly ($\underline{p}$>.10) in the frequency with which they initiated an activity or involved in an activity primary or secondary caregiving mothers. Nevertheless, infants' attachment behaviors toward primary and secondary caregiving mothers were found to differ on two dimensions. Infants displayed significantly ($\underline{p}$<.05) more affection toward primary caregiving mothers than they did toward secondary caregiving mothers. By contrast, they moved away less often ($\underline{p}$<.10) from primary caregiving mothers than they did from secondary caregiving mothers.

Table 4.19
Mothers' Caregiving Role Effects on Infants' Behaviors in a Nonstressful Situation

	Prim	Mo	Second	Mo		
	$\underline{n}$ = 14		$\underline{n}$ = 14			
Affiliative Behavior	Mean	SD	Mean	SD	$\underline{t(26)}$	Prob
Initiates Activity	5.11	2.82	6.68	2.31	1.61	–
Involves Parent	5.43	2.14	7.04	2.91	-1.67	–
Attachment Behavior						
Displays Affection	.29	.51	.00	.00	2.10	.05
Moves Away	4.29	2.87	6.32	3.46	-1.69	.10

Notes: Prim Mo = Primary Caregiving Mothers; Second Mo = Secondary Caregiving Mothers. Infants' behavior coding ranged from 0 to 30 time segments. All significance levels exceeding $\underline{p}$>.10 are indicated by dashes (–).

In summary, under nonstressful conditions infants usually exhibit similar affiliative and attachment behaviors toward caregivers of the same gender who assumed different caregiving duties. The frequency with which infants resisted the parent's activity, played with the parent or alone, looked at the parent, smiled or laughed, and vocalized in the presence of primary or secondary caregiving fathers and in the presence of primary or secondary caregiving mothers did not significantly differ. Similarly, infants did not significantly differ in the frequency with which they exhibited the attachment behaviors of approaching, being in proximity, and clinging in the presence of their primary or secondary caregiving fathers and mothers. By contrast, a caregiver role effect was observed on infants' affiliative behaviors of initiating an activity and involving parent in an activity when in the presence of fathers but not in that of mothers. Infants more often involved and initiated an activity when in the presence of primary than when in the presence of secondary caregiving fathers. The present finding suggests that primary caregiving fathers exhibited a more synchronous interaction with their infant than did secondary caregiving fathers. These differences were not observed between primary and secondary caregiving mothers. These findings are supported by the interview data, which indicate that although primary caregiving fathers assumed numerous caregiving tasks, they continued to center their interaction around playing and being involved in their infant's activity. By contrast, despite their willingness to do so, secondary caregiving fathers had little time to play with their infant when they come back from work.

Main role effects were observed on infants' attachment behaviors of displaying affection, moving away, and exploring. Infants displayed more affection toward primary than toward secondary caregivers (fathers and mothers). They also moved away more often from primary than from secondary caregiving fathers. The reverse pattern occurred in the presence of mothers. Infants moved away less often from primary than from secondary caregiving mothers.

Gender X Role Interaction Effects on Infants' Affiliative and Attachment Behaviors

Examination of the analysis of variance performed on infants' behavior (Table 4.15) indicates a gender X role effect on infants' affiliative behaviors—initiating an activity ($F[1,52] = 12.34$, $p<.001$), and involving parent in an activity ($F[1,52] = 17.05$, $p<.0001$). An interaction effect was also observed on the infants' attachment behaviors moving away

(F[1,52] = 7.27, p<.009), exploring objects (F[1,52] = 3.84, p<.055), and clinging (F[1,52] = 4.45, p<.04).

Pairwise comparisons including mean frequencies, standard deviations, and t tests were performed to explore in more detail the sources of gender X role interaction effect on infants' behavior in a nonstressful situation.

Table 4.20 shows significant differences in infants' behaviors toward primary caregiving fathers and secondary caregiving mothers within nontraditional families. Table 4.21 shows significant differences in infants' behaviors toward secondary caregiving fathers and primary caregiving mothers within traditional families.

Table 4.20
Differences of Infants' Behaviors toward Each Parent in Nontraditional Families in a Nonstressful Situation

	Prim	**Fa**	**Second**	**Mo**		
	n = 14		n = 14			
Affiliative Behavior	Mean	SD	Mean	SD	t(26)	Prob
Initiates Activity	8.54	3.34	6.68	2.31	1.71	.10
Involves Parent	9.89	4.06	7.04	2.91	2.14	.04
Attachment Behavior						
Displays Affection	.36	.50	.00	.00	2.69	.02

Note: Prim Fa = Primary Caregiving Fathers; Second Mo = Secondary Caregiving Mothers. Infants' behavior coding ranged from 0 to 30 time segments.

As indicated in Table 4.20, infants from nontraditional families displayed significantly (p<.02) more affection toward primary caregiving fathers than they did toward secondary caregiving mothers. They also more often (p<.04) involved in their activity and slightly (p<.10) more often initiated an activity when in the presence of their primary caregiving father than they did when in the presence of their secondary caregiving mother.

By contrast, as shown in Table 4.21, infants from more-traditional families displayed slightly but not significantly (p<.09) more affection toward their primary caregiving mother than they did toward their secondary caregiving father. However, they did not differ (p>.10) significantly in the frequency with which they initiated an activity or involved in an activity their primary caregiving mother or secondary caregiving father.

Table 4.21
Differences of Infants' Behaviors toward Each Parent in Traditional Families in a Nonstressful Situation

	Second	Fa	Prim	Mo		
	n = 14		n = 14			
Affiliative Behavior	Mean	SD	Mean	SD	t(26)	Prob
Initiates Activity	5.07	2.08	5.11	2.82	-.04	–
Involves Parent	5.04	2.19	5.43	2.14	-.48	–
Attachment Behavior						
Displays Affection	.04	.13	.29	.51	-1.78	.09

Notes: Second Fa = Secondary Caregiving Fathers; Prim Mo = Primary Caregiving Mothers. Infants' behavior coding ranged from 0 to 30 time segments. All t tests whose significance level exceeded p>.10 are indicated by dashes (–).

Table 4.22
Comparison of Infants' Attachment Behaviors in the Presence of Nontraditional versus Traditional Parents in a Nonstressful Situation

	Nontrad	Fam	Trad	Fam		
	n = 28		n = 28			
	Mean	SD	Mean	SD	F(1, 54)	Sig
Attachment Behavior						
Moves Away	6.38	3.09	4.29	2.58	7.55	.008
Explores Objects	6.55	3.05	5.07	2.49	3.97	.05
Clings or Climbs	.16	.36	.95	1.91	4.57	.04

Notes: Nontrad Fam = Nontraditional Families; Trad Fam = Traditional Families. Infants' behavior coding ranged from 0 to 30 time segments.

As shown in Table 4.22, the differences between infants from nontraditional and traditional families become more obvious when infants' attachment behaviors toward both of their nontraditional parents are taken as a group and compared to infants' attachment behaviors toward both of their traditional parents taken as a group. By comparison to infants from traditional families, infants from nontraditional families more often moved away from, more often explored, and less often clung to either one of their parents. These differences were all found to be significant ($p < .05$).

Summary and Conclusion: Caregiver Gender and Caregiving Role Effects on Infants' Behaviors in a Nonstressful Situation

The lack of gender, role, or interaction effect on most of infants' affiliative behaviors indicates that in a nonstressful situation infants did not significantly differ in the frequency with which they smiled, looked, vocalized, played, or resisted activities of caregivers of different gender and assuming different caregiving duties.

More-focused comparisons performed with t tests showed the influence of the caregiver gender on some of the infants' affiliative behaviors. Infants were found to more often involve in an activity and to more often initiate an activity in the presence of fathers than in the presence of mothers who assumed primary caregiving duties. Yet, the caregiving role fathers assumed also influenced these measures. Infants more often involved in an activity and more often initiated an activity in the presence of primary than in that of secondary caregiving fathers. The gender X role interaction observed on some of the infants' affiliative behaviors—initiating an activity and involving parent in an activity—also suggests that more than any other category of caregivers, primary caregiving fathers were adept at getting involved in their infant's activity and at letting their infant initiate an activity in their presence. Therefore, primary caregiving fathers displayed the greatest synchronous interaction with their infants. These findings are supported by the interview data, which indicated that despite the numerous caregiving tasks they had to assume, primary caregiving fathers continued to center their interaction with their infant around play. They took the time to get involved in their infant's play or simply enjoyed watching their infant initiate new activities.

When considering infants' attachment behaviors in a nonstressful situation, a caregiving role effect was observed on displaying affection and a gender X role interaction effect was observed on clinging, moving away, and exploring from a secure base. Already under nonstressful conditions, when specific attachment behaviors are focused upon, such as displaying affection, the primacy of the caregiver role rather than the gender of the caregiver assumes a predominant influence. Thus, while disregarding the gender of their caregivers, infants displayed more affection toward the parent who took care of them for the greatest part of the day, that is, their primary caregiver.

Under nonstressful conditions, infants in nontraditional families were also found to more often move away, to more often explore, and to less often cling to either one of their parents than did infants in more traditional families. By these criteria, in a nonstressful situation infants cared for by nontraditional parents exhibited less-anxious attachment behaviors toward their parents than did infants cared for by more traditional parents. Thus, they felt more at ease to explore their environment while in the presence of either one of their parents or a stranger.

ANALYSIS OF INFANTS' AFFILIATIVE AND ATTACHMENT BEHAVIORS IN A STRESSFUL SITUATION

The third research question aimed at finding out toward which one of the parents, both present in the same room, would most infants' attachment behaviors be directed under stress. To answer this question, infants were observed in a modified version of the Strange Situation. In episode 3, infants were put under increasing levels of stress when asked to play with a stranger and when picked up by that stranger. Both of the parents remained seated at opposite sides of the stranger. This procedure was expected to last five minutes. However, in some cases infants became too stressed when experiencing physical contact with the stranger. Their screaming and crying necessitated the parents' intervention and the interruption of the observation. As a result, some infants were observed for five minutes and others for less. The minimum observation time was three minutes. A different method of scoring than fifteen time-sampled periods had to be adopted in order to adjust for the fact that the infants who were observed longer were obtaining misleadingly higher scores under stress. Therefore, all infants' affiliative and attachment behaviors observed under stress were scored as percentage of time a behavior occurred during the coding periods before episode 3 was terminated.

Distress Levels Experienced

Table 4.23 shows no significant differences in the overt indicators of distress experienced by infants from nontraditional and traditional families. In both family types, infants were similar in the amount of time they could tolerate being held by a stranger and in the percentage of time segments in which they whined or screamed under stress.

Table 4.23
Comparison of Distress Indicators for Infants from Traditional and Nontraditional Families in a Stressful Situation

	Nontrad	Fam	Trad	Fam		
	$\underline{n} = 28$		$\underline{n} = 28$			
Indicators of Distress	Mean	SD	Mean	SD	t(26)	Prob
Stranger Holds Baby	26.39	10.56	28.43	9.55	–	–
Whines	8.64	13.81	9.79	10.35	–	–
Screams	11.46	19.76	13.57	21.64	–	–

Notes: Trad Fam = Traditional Families; Nontrad Fam = Nontraditional These behaviors were coded in percentage of time they occurred during the coding periods before episode 3 was terminated. All significance levels exceeding p>.10 are indicated by dashes (–).

Infants' Affiliative Behavior under Stress

Infants' affiliative behaviors—joins stranger activity, smiles or laughs, and vocalizes—as well as their negative indicators—ignores, plays alone, and physically resists—were coded as percentage of time segments they occurred during the coding periods before episode 3 was terminated (Table 4.24).

Although both parents were present during all of this episode, it was not always possible to specify toward whom (father, mother, or stranger) these affiliative behaviors were directed. Infants often laughed, smiled, or vocalized during episode 3 without specifically orienting their smile or vocalization toward either one of their parents or toward the stranger. Therefore, the only comparisons that could be made were those of infants' affiliative behaviors under stress in the presence of both nontraditional parents and a stranger versus those in the presence of both traditional parents and a stranger. Under the same level of stress created by interaction with a stranger, there were no significant differences (p>.10) between the affiliative behaviors of infants cared for by nontraditional parents and those of infants cared for by more traditional parents. Under stress, infants in both family types were similar in the percentage of time segments during which they joined or resisted the stranger's activity, played with the stranger or alone, smiled or vocalized (Table 4.24).

Table 4.24
**Comparison of the Affiliative Behaviors under Stress of Infants
from Nontraditional and Traditional Families**

Affiliative Behavior	Nontrad Fam n = 28		Trad Fam n = 28			
	Mean	SD	Mean	SD	t(26)	Prob
Toward Stranger						
Joins	45.21	30.48	37.96	22.01	–	–
Ignores	19.98	16.44	24.96	16.30	–	–
Plays Alone	5.86	8.01	7.45	6.75	–	–
Physically Resists	14.71	17.14	16.50	11.78	–	–
Toward Parent/Stranger						
Smiles or Laughs	15.86	13.25	17.09	10.00	–	–
Vocalizes	22.16	15.72	18.36	13.83	–	–

Notes: Trad Fam = Traditional Families; Nontrad Fam = Nontraditional Families.
These behaviors were coded in percentage of time they occurred during the coding
periods before episode 3 was terminated. All significance levels exceeded $p > .10$
are indicated by dashes (–).

Infants' Attachment Behaviors under Stress

In episode 3, the seating arrangement of the parents and the behavioral
definitions of infants' attachment behaviors under stress were such that
infants could direct these behaviors to one parent at a time but not to both. It
was thus possible at the coding stage to record toward which parent the
attachment behaviors—staying in proximity, approaching, looking, turning
their body toward, and seeking or resisting physical contact—were directed.
A caregiver gender X caregiving role analysis of variance was performed on
each of the dependent measures of infants' attachment behavior under stress.
This analysis concerned the relative frequency with which infants displayed
attachment behaviors toward each recipient parent categorized according to
his or her gender and role (Table 4.25).

Effect of Caregiver Gender on Infants' Attachment Behaviors under Stress

The analysis of variance performed in Table 4.25 indicates a lack of caregiver gender effect on all infants' attachment behaviors under stress—in proximity to one of the parents, approaching one of the parents, turning body towards one of the parents, looking at one of the parents, physical contact with one of the parents, and resisting one of the parents. All infants' behaviors under stress were then combined into one measure of attachment under stress. The analysis of variance performed in Table 4.26 shows no gender effect on this composite.

Table 4.25
Influence of Caregiver Gender and Caregiving Role on Infants' Attachment Behaviors under Stress: ANOVA

	Gender		Role		Gender X	Role
Attachment Behavior	**F(1,52)**	**Sig**	**F(1,52)**	**Sig**		
In Proximity	–	–	20.11	.0001	–	–
Approaches Parent	–	–	21.75	.0001	–	–
Body Turned to Parent	–	–	44.65	.0001	–	–
Looks at Parent	–	–	54.84	.0001	–	–
Physical Contact	–	–	13.46	.001	–	–
Resists Parent	–	–	2.91	.09	–	–

Note: All F tests whose significance level exceeded $p > .10$ are indicated by dashes (–).

Effect of Caregiver Role on Infants' Attachment Behaviors under Stress

Examination of the analysis of variance performed on infants' attachment behaviors under stress (Table 4.25) indicates a main role effect on being in proximity to one of the parents ($F[1,52] = 20.11$, $p < .0001$), approaching one parent ($F[1,52] = 21.75$, $p < .0001$), turning body toward one parent ($F[1,52] = 44.65$, $p < .0001$), looking at one parent ($F[1,52] = 54.84$, $p < .0001$), and physical contact with one of the parents ($F[1,52] = 13.46$, $p < .001$). A main role effect was also observed (Table 4.26) on the composite measure of attachment under stress ($F[1,52] = 39.63$, $p < .0001$) which was found to explain a significant proportion of the variance ($r = .65$).

Table 4.26
Influence of Caregiver Gender and Caregiving Role on the
Composites of Infants' Attachment Behaviors under Stress: ANOVA

	Gender		Role		Gender X Role	
Composite	F(1,52)	Sig	F(1,52)	Sig	F(1,52)	Sig
Attachment–Stress	–	–	39.63	.0001	–	–
(In proximity + turns						
+ approaches + looks						
+ picked up - resists)						

Note: All F tests exceeding p>.10 are indicated by dashes (–).

Table 4.27 categorizes infants' attachment behaviors under stress according to the gender of the recipient parent and the nontraditional or traditional role they fulfill. It shows the mean percentage of time segments on which the analysis of variance in Table 4.25 was based. In this manner, the attachment behaviors of the infants toward fathers in nontraditional families could be compared to those displayed toward traditional fathers, and the attachment behaviors that infants displayed in the presence of nontraditional mothers could be compared to those displayed in the presence of traditional mothers.

As indicated in Table 4.27, in a stressful situation created by contact with a stranger, infants in nontraditional families more often stayed in proximity, approached, looked at, turned their bodies toward, and sought physical contact of their father than did infants in more-traditional families. By contrast, infants in nontraditional families less often stayed in proximity, approached, looked at, turned their bodies toward, and sought physical contact of their mother than did infants in traditional families. Thus, under stress, by comparison to infants from traditional families, infants from nontraditional families more often directed their attachment behavior toward their father and less often toward their mother.

By making comparisons within rather than between families and thus comparing the data of Table 4.27 down the columns rather than across the rows, it may be observed whether, under stress, infants directed their attachment behaviors toward their mother or their father. Table 4.28 shows comparisons between fathers and mothers within nontraditional families, while Table 4.29 allows the same comparisons within traditional families.

Table 4.27
Comparison of Infants' Attachment Behaviors under Stress toward Each Parent in Traditional and Nontraditional Families

Attachment Behavior	Nontrad Fam n = 28 Mean	SD	Trad Fam n = 28 Mean	SD	t(26)	Prob
In Proximity to						
father	19.11	17.64	4.82	5.05	2.91	.01
mother	5.32	13.20	25.07	17.19	-3.41	.002
Approaches/Goes to						
father	10.43	9.71	4.04	3.33	2.33	.03
mother	3.68	4.52	13.64	6.82	-4.56	.00
Looks at						
father	27.25	17.91	5.43	5.38	4.37	.001
mother	5.04	6.58	35.29	17.30	-6.11	.000
Body Turned to						
father	29.50	22.67	3.89	3.77	4.17	.001
mother	6.21	10.20	38.54	20.50	-5.28	.000
Physical Contact with						
father	17.00	18.94	2.71	4.61	2.74	.02
mother	4.43	7.41	16.43	16.84	-2.44	.03
Physically Resists						
father	.00	.00	2.07	4.28	-1.81	.09
mother	.57	1.47	.50	1.27	.14	–

Notes: Nontrad Fam = Nontraditional Families; Trad Fam = Traditional Families.
These behaviors were coded in percentage of time they occurred during the coding periods before episode was terminated. All significance levels exceeding $p > .10$ are indicated by dashes (–).

Table 4.28
Comparison of Infants' Attachment Behaviors under Stress toward Each Parent in Nontraditional Families

| | Prim | Fa | Second | Mo | | |
| | n = 14 | | n = 14 | | | |
Attachment Behavior	Mean	SD	Mean	SD	t(26)	Prob
In Proximity	19.11	17.64	5.32	13.20	2.34	.03
Approaches/Goes to	10.43	9.71	3.68	4.52	2.36	.03
Looks at Parent	27.25	17.91	5.04	6.58	4.36	.000
Body Turned toward	29.50	22.67	6.21	10.20	3.51	.003
Physical Contact	17.00	18.94	7.40	7.40	2.31	.03
Physically Resists	.00	.00	.57	1.47	-1.46	—

Notes: Prim Fa = Primary Caregiving Fathers; Second Mo = Secondary Caregiving Mothers. These behaviors were coded in percentage of time they occurred during the coding periods before episode 3 was terminated. All significance levels exceeding $p > .10$ are indicated by dashes (–).

As shown in Table 4.28, under stress and when they had the choice between their father and their mother, infants in nontraditional families more often directed toward primary caregiving fathers than towards secondary caregiving mothers all the attachment behaviors coded in this study—staying in proximity, approaching, looking, turned body toward, and seeking physical contact.

By contrast, as shown in Table 4.29, this pattern of preference is reversed for infants from more-traditional families. These infants more often directed toward primary caregiving mothers than toward secondary caregiving fathers all the attachment behaviors coded in this study—staying in proximity, approaching, looking, turning body toward, and seeking physical contact.

Table 4.29
Comparison of Infants' Attachment Behaviors under Stress toward
Each Parent in Traditional Families

Attachment Behavior	Second Fa n = 14 Mean	SD	Prim Mo n = 14 Mean	SD	t(26)	Prob
In Proximity	4.82	5.05	25.07	17.19	-4.23	.000
Approaches/Goes to	4.04	3.33	13.64	6.82	-4.74	.000
Looks at Parent	5.43	5.38	35.29	17.30	-6.17	.000
Body Turned toward	3.89	3.77	38.54	20.50	-6.22	.000
Physical Contact	2.71	4.61	16.43	16.84	-2.94	.01
Physically Resists	2.07	4.28	.50	1.27	1.32	–

Notes: Second Fa = Secondary Caregiving Father; Prim Mo = Primary Caregiving
Mothers. These behaviors were coded in percentage of time they occurred during the
coding periods before episode 3 was terminated. All significance levels exceeding
p>.10 are indicated by dashes (–).

Summary of Caregiver Gender and Caregiving Role Effects on Infants' Attachment Behaviors under Stress

A main role effect was observed on all infants' attachment behaviors
under stress—remaining in proximity to one of the parents, approaching one
of the parents, turning body toward one of the parents, looking at one of the
parents, and physical contact with one of the parents. No gender or
interaction effect was observed on any of these attachment measures. The
attachment behaviors under stress of infants from traditional and
nontraditional families toward caregivers of the same gender but assuming
different caregiving roles, and toward caregivers of different gender who
assumed the same caregiving roles were also examined. The results of this
comparison indicate that under stress infants more often directed their
attachment behaviors toward primary than toward secondary caregiving
fathers. Similarly, infants more often directed attachment behaviors toward
primary than toward secondary caregiving mothers. Furthermore, whenever
they had the choice between their father and their mother, infants directed

most of their attachment behaviors toward their father when their father was the primary caregiver, as was the case in nontraditional families, or toward their mother when their mother was the primary caregiver, as was the case in more-traditional families. Thus, under stress, infants did not prefer their mother to their father. They preferred and directed most of their attachment behaviors toward the parent who had picked them up, comforted them, and assumed the sole responsibility of their care for most part of the day—their primary caregiver—with total disregard for their gender.

NOTE

1. Gender of the caregiver X primacy of the caregiver role means the interaction effect of the gender of the caregiver with the caregiving role of the caregiver.

5

Discussion: Primary Caregiving Fathers and Egalitarian Upbringing

In this study the affiliative and attachment behaviors of nontraditional fathers who have become their infant's primary caregivers have been examined. These fathers have been compared to more-traditional secondary caregiving fathers and to primary and secondary caregiving mothers. The common characteristic of these various categories of caregivers was that they wanted their infants to be cared for at home by one of the parents when the other parent was at work. So, while secondary caregiving mothers in nontraditional families and secondary caregiving fathers in more-traditional families were employed full-time outside the home, their spouse assumed during the day primary caregiving duties by taking care of their infant.

Despite the similarities just mentioned, there were differences in the child-care arrangements adopted by the two family types. Interview data revealed that in nontraditional families most of the primary caregiving fathers worked outside the home more than half time and thus used, during the day, the regular services of a babysitter for up to fifteen hours a week. By contrast, in traditional families primary caregiving mothers were during the day their infant's exclusive caregivers. The only time they hired a babysitter was to go out at night, once or twice a month.

Another difference noted was the length of time the actual arrangement had been adopted. In nontraditional families, the majority of the fathers had become primary caregivers when their infant was between four and eight months of age. Until then, secondary caregiving mothers had assumed primary caregiving duties while on maternity leave of absence that enabled them to take care of their infant during the day. By contrast, in traditional families mothers had abandoned their career at the birth of their infant to become their infant's primary caregiver.

INTERVIEW DATA

Attitude and Motivation

Several factors combine to explain why nontraditional and traditional parents alike had adopted this specific type of child-care arrangement. These include the parents' attitudes toward child care and day care and their motivation to take care of their infant, their educational background, their employment potential and work schedule, as well as their beliefs about the roles men and women play in child care.

Based on their perceptions of infants' psychological needs for personal attention and for a parent to be around them, parents in nontraditional and traditional families did not believe that day care was an option for infants at such a young age. Furthermore, parents who assumed primary caregiving duties were always highly motivated to take care of their infants. Primary caregiving mothers loved to be mothers and primary caregiving fathers felt that taking care of their infant was a unique experience they did not want to miss.

Educational Level

The educational level of parents in both nontraditional and traditional families was high. Most of the parents in both family types had college degrees. Based on the criteria of education and occupation, the research participants could be categorized as middle-class professionals. Primary caregiving fathers were college professors, lawyers, or graduate students who enjoyed flexible work hours. They could schedule their working hours around taking care of their infants. However, although secondary caregiving fathers in the present study were self-employed professionals, that is, dentists, physicians, or business owners, they did not have too much leeway in scheduling their work hours. Both categories of caregiving fathers had, nonetheless, come to rethink the values of professional achievement and success versus parenthood and family life. Primary and secondary caregiving fathers had both realized the importance of parenthood, but primary caregiving fathers were less career oriented than were secondary caregiving fathers. Secondary caregiving mothers were career oriented and usually employed in highly paid positions, whereas primary caregiving mothers had temporarily abandoned their careers to take care of their infant full-time.

Beliefs Concerning the Role of Men and Women in Child Care

Nontraditional and traditional parents' high level of education seemed to have exposed them to recent trends concerning the importance of fathers in infants' development and dissipated their stereotypes about the role of men and women in child care. In both family types, primary and secondary caregiving mothers and fathers believed that parents should share caregiving duties. However, the meaning of sharing varied according to the family type. Primary caregiving mothers believed that it was fair to assume all caregiving and household tasks during the day since their spouse was the only breadwinner and worked full-time outside the home. They also believed, and so did their spouse, that once at home, secondary caregiving fathers should assume an equal share of child-care responsibilities. By contrast, both parents in nontraditional families believed that each parent should assume an equal share of responsibilities inside and outside the home.

Satisfaction with Child Care

Primary caregiving fathers expressed satisfaction of being deeply involved with their infant, while playing with them, or simply watching them grow. And although sarcasm about "Mr. Mom" and lack of understanding had at times been confronted by secondary caregiving mothers at work, the support of their bosses and the positive reaction of significant others had reinforced primary caregiving fathers' satisfaction with the child-care arrangement they had adopted.

Patterns of Sharing

Interview data about the way caregiving duties were actually shared when both parents were at home in the evenings and on weekends indicated that nontraditional families in which fathers were the primary caregivers were more egalitarian than the reference group of traditional families. When both parents were at home, between 64 to 94 percent of primary caregiving fathers, as opposed to up to 50 percent of secondary caregiving fathers, reported sharing equally with their spouse the tasks of bathing, feeding, diapering, comforting, and putting the baby to sleep. Also, whenever these duties were not shared, they were generally assumed by primary caregiving fathers in nontraditional families and by primary caregiving mothers in traditional families.

Portrayal of Secondary Caregiving Fathers

Despite the differences noted between primary and secondary caregiving fathers, interview data indicate that the portrayal of secondary caregiving fathers as working all day, barely seeing their infant, and rarely committed or involved in caregiving or play depicted in some literature of the past twenty-five years (Kotelchuck, 1976; Russel, 1983) is no longer accurate and no longer represents American fathers. Once at home, most of the secondary caregiving fathers in the sample did play with their infant and did assume numerous caregiving responsibilities such as diapering, feeding, and putting the baby to sleep. In fact, it was almost impossible to find secondary caregiving fathers who were not involved in caregiving. Some primary caregiving mothers complained that their spouse was not sufficiently committed to child rearing, while others complained that their spouse worked too much outside the house and thus could not help as much as he otherwise would have had he been at home. But no primary caregiving mother complained that her spouse refused to change diapers or to play with their infant.

Effect of Caregiver Gender and Caregiving Role on Sharing

Interview data indicate that the amount of caregiving duties assumed was based on the caregiving role rather than on the gender of the caregiver. Even though secondary caregiving fathers or mothers reported sharing once at home, the primary caregivers (fathers and mothers) continued to assume a greater share of caregiving responsibilities. The exception concerns the task of getting up at night for which the gender of the caregiver rather than the caregiving role assumed greater influence. The task of getting up at night remained predominantly mothers' job, apparently because of the baby's need to nurse.

Similarly, although all parents spent some time interacting with their infant, the amount of interaction time was, in absolute terms, influenced by the caregiving role rather than the caregiver gender. Secondary caregiving fathers and mothers had, obviously, less opportunity to interact with their infant. Once they came back from work at 6 P.M. it was dinner time, followed by a short play period, and then bedtime for the baby. By contrast, and consistent with past research findings, the play style and attitude toward play were based on the gender of the caregiver rather than on the caregiving role assumed. Whether primary or secondary caregivers, fathers were more relaxed with their infant and more fully involved in play with their infant than mothers were. Primary and secondary caregiving mothers usually interacted in play with their infant while busy performing other chores.

OBSERVATIONAL DATA

Influence of Caregiver Gender and Caregiving Role on Caregivers' Behaviors

Under nonstressful conditions, primary and secondary caregiving fathers and mothers have been found to exhibit similar affiliative behaviors toward their infant. Whatever the caregiver gender or caregiving role assumed, the frequency with which parents looked, talked, and played with their infant did not differ significantly. The exception concerns rough-and-tumble play, on which a significant gender effect was observed with fathers who demonstrated more of this type of interaction.

Differences based on the caregiving role assumed were observed on the attachment behaviors of the various categories of caregivers. Whatever their gender (father or mother), primary caregivers displayed more affection toward their infant than did secondary caregivers. Primary caregiving fathers were also found to be the most affectionate caregivers. They hugged and kissed their infant more frequently than any other category of caregivers did.

Primary caregiving fathers were also able to combine affection and child care with rough-and-tumble play, which constituted a pleasurable and exciting experience to the child. Primary caregiving fathers' play style remained similar to that of secondary caregiving fathers while differing from that of primary and secondary caregiving mothers. The rough-and-tumble play style of fathers in the United States was therefore unaffected by the caregiving role fathers assumed.

Influence of Caregiver Gender and Caregiving Role on Infants' Behaviors in a Nonstressful Situation

Under nonstressful conditions, infants displayed similar affiliative behaviors toward caregivers of different gender and assuming different caregiving roles. The frequency with which infants smiled, looked, vocalized, played, or resisted activities did not differ significantly in the presence of the various categories of caregivers. A caregiver gender X caregiving role interaction effect was observed in the synchronous interaction between the parent and the infant under nonstressful conditions. Infants initiated an activity and involved in their activity more often their primary caregiving father than any other category of caregivers. Primary caregiving fathers and infants in their presence were most attuned to each other's play behavior.

Past research has indicated infants' affiliative preference for their father over mother. The concept of "quality time" interaction has been introduced to explain infants' preference for fathers over mothers even though infants were spending less time with their father. This study shows that the many hours primary caregiving fathers were spending involved with their infant allowed for a greater understanding of the nuances in their infant's behavior, for prompt and mutual responding, and thus for a greater degree of synchrony. An important implication of this finding is therefore that parents cannot expect to give "quality time" without simultaneously investing "quantity of time" interacting one-to-one with their infant.

The primacy of the caregiver role rather than the gender of the caregiver was already found to assume a predominant influence on specific attachment behaviors of the infants under nonstressful conditions. While disregarding their gender (father or mother), infants displayed more affection toward the parent who had taken care of them for the greatest part of the day, namely, their primary caregiver. The caregiver gender X role interaction effect observed on the attachment behaviors—clinging, moving away, and exploring from a secure base—indicated that infants cared for by primary caregiving fathers in nontraditional families displayed less-anxious attachment than did infants cared for by primary caregiving mothers in traditional families. They, thus, felt more free and autonomous while exploring their environment in the presence of either one of their nontraditional parents and a stranger.

Influence of Caregiving Role on Infants' Attachment Behaviors under Stress

Once under stress and based on all infants' attachment behaviors, the preference toward primary caregivers emerged more powerfully with disregard for their gender. Under stress, when they had the choice between their parents, infants more often approached, stayed in proximity to, looked at, turned their body towards, and sought physical contact of their father when their father was the primary caregiver, as was the case in nontraditional families, or of their mother when their mother was the primary caregiver, as was the case of traditional families. By these criteria, infants invariably preferred the parent who had provided them with care and affection for the greatest part of the day, with total disregard for their gender.

GENDER DIFFERENCES IN PARENTING

The results of this study concerning the predominant influence of the caregiving role on caregivers' and infants' behaviors conflict with the findings of Frodi and her colleagues (1983). After observing a main gender effect and a lack of role effect on parental behavior, Frodi and her colleagues (1983) commented that perhaps greater paternal involvement in child care than the one they had required from their research participants was needed to eliminate "gender differences in the style of parental behavior" (Frodi et al., 1983, p. 159) in order to observe differences based on the caregiving role assumed.

The findings of the current study support this comment and indicate that the criterion of Frodi and her colleagues, "spending on the average of 3 months as primary caretakers," (1983, p. 159) was not a sufficient indication of paternal involvement. This is especially the case in their study because although the father participants had planned to become actively involved in child care and to assume primary caregiving duties for at least three months, their actual involvement at the time of the first observation averaged only one month. This length of time was, obviously, too brief to allow for the qualitative changes in father-infant interaction that would result from fathers' greater involvement in child care. Furthermore, Swedish fathers' commitment to being primary caregivers was temporary. They knew that they would be at home for only a limited period of time and expected to return to work soon afterwards. Such limited commitment did not result in role change (Lamb & Levine, 1983). By contrast, based on the behavior of fathers who had assumed primary caregiving duties for a period longer than three months, the findings of the current study, as well as cross-cultural interview data (Defrain, 1979; Field, 1978; Gronseth, 1975; Radin, 1980; Russel, 1983), indicate a consistent effect of the primacy of the caregiving role and a minimal if not nonexistent gender effect on caregivers' behaviors.

Primary and secondary caregiving fathers participating in the present study were found willing and able to change diapers, feed, bathe, and put their infant to sleep. Primary caregiving fathers assumed as many caregiving duties as primary or secondary caregiving mothers did. They were also the most-affectionate caregivers. As indicated by the interview data, despite increased child-care responsibilities, primary caregiving fathers continued to dedicate most of their time to play and were not as concerned as primary caregiving mothers were about housecleaning and related chores. Finally, primary caregiving fathers were more in synchrony with their infant's activities than any other category of caregivers.

These findings suggest that gender differences in parenting are minimal and result from differences in child-care involvement. Daily participation in child care in the role of primary caregiver increases fathers' experience, skill, and confidence as caregivers. Increased competence and involvement lead to qualitative changes in the father-infant relationship. By watching their infants grow, enjoying their first steps and first spoken words, and being there at critical moments, primary caregiving fathers could enjoy a closer and more intimate relationship with their infant.

The findings of the present study also suggest that parents' behavior in child care is indeed amenable to sociocultural influence. Just as the rough-and-tumble play style of U.S. primary and secondary fathers alike is distinctive from that of Swedish fathers and under the influence of these respective cultures (Frodi et al., 1983), so are fathers' nurturing and caregiving behaviors under social influences and depend on the social role assumed. For example, the traditional stereotypes held by many employers in Sweden concerning men's and women's role in child care have discouraged fathers from taking a leave of absence despite advanced family policies and legislation entitling them to such a leave (Lamb & Levine, 1983). By contrast, the support of their bosses has encouraged American fathers participating in the current study to retain their primary caregiving role.

Primary caregiving fathers did engage in behaviors, such as kissing and hugging, that in the past were considered to be behaviors typical of mothers. By contrast, these behaviors have been found to be greatly reduced in mothers who assumed secondary caregiving duties. Primary caregiving fathers were also found to be more attuned to their infant's behavior than were secondary caregiving mothers and fathers and primary caregiving mothers because they were spending more time involved with their infant in play. This finding once more indicates that the primacy of the caregiving role assumed as well as the time invested and experience with the infant are determinant factors in influencing the caregiver's behaviors.

ATTACHMENT THEORIES REVISITED

These findings refute Freud's (1948) contention that "infants' sucking for nourishment" is at the basis of all subsequent attachment relationships. Hull's drive reduction hypothesis (1943), that mothers acquire the value of a secondary reinforcer by satisfying their infant's hunger drive, has been disconfirmed. By contrast, Harlow's contrary hypothesis (1961) has been confirmed. This hypothesis assumed that it was not the actual feeding but the circumstances surrounding the feeding, namely, the warmth and comfort provided by the caregiver that were at the origin of the infant-mother bond.

Even though primary caregiving fathers did not nurse their infants, they could provide them the warmth and affection they needed. They had thus become a greater source of comfort to their infants than secondary caregiving mothers were. This explains why, when under stress, infants in nontraditional families preferred by all their attachment behaviors their primary caregiving father to their secondary caregiving mother.

The assumption of attachment theorists, Bowlby (1969), Ainsworth, Bell & Stayton (1974), and Lamb (1977, 1978c), that the attachment behavioral system becomes activated under stress has also been confirmed. However, another assumption of attachment theorists, namely, that under stress, a hierarchy in preference emerges with mothers preferred to fathers is valid only when qualified by adding *and under the condition that the mother is the primary caregiver and that the father is the secondary caregiver.* Infants do not prefer their mother to their father regardless of the caregiving role they assume. Infants prefer their mother to their father *only when* their mother is the primary caregiver. By contrast, they prefer their father to their mother *when* their father is the primary caregiver.

The findings that infants more often explore, move away from, and less often cling when in the presence of either one of their nontraditional parents than when in the presence of either one of their more traditional parents support the assumptions of separation-individuation theorists (Abelin, 1971, 1975; Forrest, 1967; Leonard, 1966; Mahler, Pine & Bergman, 1975; Winnicott, 1956). Based on one of these assumptions, it may be explained that primary caregiving fathers help release infants from symbiotic unity with mothers. By contrast, the exclusive care primary caregiving mothers provide to their infant and their constant presence during the day and when their spouse returns from work prevent the push toward greater autonomy.

Another assumption of separation-individuation theory that mothers provide infants with "a reservoir of basic trust" that allows them to explore the world may be modified to include primary caregiving fathers in the presence of whom infants exhibited most explorative behaviors. In Erikson's (1950) theory, trust is crucial for the acquisition of autonomy. It may thus be theorized that once they preferred their father as primary attachment figure, as was the case in nontraditional families, infants no longer feared or longed for reengulfment into unity with their mother. They also felt more free and less anxious of being separated from their mother than were infants in traditional families. They thus exhibited more autonomous exploration in the presence of either one of their nontraditional parents than did infants in the presence of either one of their traditional parents.

By the affection and caregiving behavior they display, as well as by their play interaction, primary caregiving fathers were presenting to their infant a model of friendly interaction with the social world. Thus, the presence of a stranger videotaping produced less tension and anxiety in infants cared for by nontraditional parents than in infants cared for by more-traditional parents. The reduced anxiety was once more indicated by more exploration and less clinging.

The findings of the current study support the conclusion that primary caregiving fathers could combine the roles of nurturance and affiliation that were in the past separated and exclusively attributed to either mothers or fathers. Primary caregiving fathers have become their infant's "super partners." Their testimony, and that of their spouse, indicated that they were competent in diapering, feeding, and putting the baby to sleep. They were also able to give and receive affection, while remaining exciting play partners ready to engage in boisterous play such as throwing their infant in the air, swinging the infant around, and lifting the infant upside down.

The reactions of primary caregiving fathers during the videotaping sessions suggest that they did not yet realize the central role they played in the lives of their infant. They were often embarrassed and apologetic when their infant approached them rather than their spouse to be comforted. These fathers often argued that had the seating arrangement been reversed, the child would have gone to the mother instead. At the second session, when the parents' seating position was in fact reversed, a few infants did indeed go to their mother, but the majority of infants once more sought proximity of their amazed and amazing father. Secondary caregiving mothers did not appear to be disturbed, and often seemed pleased to see that under stress their infant preferred and directed most of their attachment behaviors toward their father. These mothers had chosen to give up the primary caregiving role that society had exclusively assigned to women for generations. As secondary caregivers, mothers could dedicate more hours to their work confident that their infant was with the best caregiver they could think of: Da-ddy!

FUTURE RESEARCH ON PRIMARY CAREGIVING FATHERS

Further research is now needed to expand knowledge about the influence of primary caregiving fathers on the sociocognitive development of their children. Secondary caregiving fathers' involvement and play interaction have been found invaluable in the acquisition of social competence (Belsky, 1980). Infants' curiosity and motivation to explore the world have been associated with the frequency with which secondary caregiving fathers verbally and emotionally responded to their infants' signals as well as to the frequency with which they engaged in physical play (Belsky, 1980). Secondary caregiving fathers' involvement and play interaction were also related to toddlers' optimal sociocognitive performance. However, when compared to primary caregiving mothers, secondary caregiving fathers have been found to respond to, rather than to stimulate, their children's intellectual performance (Belsky, 1980). Further research will clarify whether primary caregiving fathers' increased involvement in child care and more frequent display of affection and play interaction could stimulate the intellectual and social development of their infant.

Another topic not addressed by this study is the effect of infants' gender on parents' and infants' behaviors. Secondary caregiving fathers have been found to be more involved with their sons, and primary caregiving mothers to be more involved with their daughters (Parke & Sawin, 1975). Fathers vocalized, touched, and responded more to their newborn sons than to their newborn daughters. By contrast, affectionate behavior has been found more frequent across parent-infant gender, that is, between mothers and sons and between fathers and daughters (Parke & O'Leary, 1976; Parke & Sawin, 1975; Rebelsky & Hanks, 1971). Reciprocally, one-year old infants have been found to look at, vocalize, fuss, and stay in proximity to the same sex parent (Ban & Lewis, 1974; Lamb, 1980; Spelke et al., 1973). Research is needed to examine whether gender differences observed in past studies on parents' and infants' behaviors continue to exist in nontraditional families composed of primary caregiving fathers and secondary caregiving mothers.

This research examined infant-father attachment in nontraditional families, in which fathers took the primary responsibility of raising their infant. Primary caregiving fathers were found to be as competent as mothers in assuming various caregiving tasks and expressing affection. This type of egalitarian child rearing opens new horizons to infants as they grow up and become adults. Socialization by role models that transcends male and female stereotypes could lead to a variety of experiences and choices in life worthy of future research efforts.

LIMITATIONS OF THIS STUDY

The behavioral definitions adopted in this study have been based on those used in past research. There were many different categories for affiliative behaviors, especially for various kinds of play in which parents engaged with their infant. By contrast, the behavioral categories for parents' attachment behavior were few and amounted to caregiving and displaying affection. Further research is needed to refine and expand parents' attachment behavioral categories in order to include a measure of mutual responding, being attuned to the signals of their infant, and a measure of competence in caregiving.

During the interviews some of the primary caregiving mothers commented that they had played more with their first born than with their second born. Other mothers commented that they had picked up their infants much more often before they had started to walk. As a consequence of these comments, other topics of interest that have not been addressed by this research emerge, namely, whether infants' and parents' affiliative and attachment behavior toward each other vary depending on the infant's birth order (first versus second born) or on the infant's developmental capabilities.

IMPLICATIONS OF THIS STUDY

Waiting for these topics to be explored, the results of the current study present far reaching political and social implications. In the past, fathers who assumed primary caregiving duties were presumed to do so out of economic necessity, because they were too poor to afford day care. They were college students, or workers who had to rotate shifts with their spouse (Lamb & Levine, 1983). Today, primary caregiving fathers can no longer be written off as eccentric—they have become an integral part of the middle-class social reality. In fact, in 1991, fathers taking care of infants under one year of age in the home constituted the most common form of child-care arrangement adopted by employed mothers.[1]

As women are becoming more educated and able to participate in the labor force as professionals, they no longer feel excluded from the domain that used to be exclusively that of men (professional work) or confined to the domain that used to be uniquely assigned to women (child care). Many request that obligations be shared equally inside and outside the home.

Thus, fathers who share at least half of primary caregiving duties have become the precursors of real socioeconomic equality between women and men. In the words of Russel (1983), "It is child care, however, that is probably the most demanding and constant of family work tasks, and it is the divisions of labour for child care and associated beliefs about parental roles that form the basis of sexual divisions in other domains" (p. 53).

This study suggests broad attitudinal and ideological shifts concerning gender-role definitions, alternative formulations of fathers' roles, and correlative dissipation of traditional stereotypes. Fathers can no longer be defined by their educational, occupational, or socioeconomic status they have attained for their family. Fathers' ability to nurture, kiss, hug, and express affection, as well as their ability to respond and synchronize their behavior with that of their infant, have to be acknowledged and included in the concept of fatherhood. A new definition of father that includes nurturant, expressive, and affiliative dimensions of fatherhood would legitimize a more androgynous type of parenting and interchangeability between fathers' and mothers' roles.

The culturally defined set of expectations concerning the role and appropriate behaviors of each family member used to be based on gender. The current study presents alternative expressions of what constitutes fathers' and mothers' roles and behaviors based on the caregiving role assumed. At one end of the continuum may be found traditional fathers who are the breadwinners and secondary caregivers, coupled with traditional mothers who are their infant's exclusive caregivers. At the other end of the continuum may be found nontraditional fathers who assume primary caregiving duties and household chores while their spouse is employed full-time outside the home. Midway along this continuum are located fathers and mothers who share equally outside employment and caregiving responsibilities.

Fathers have become increasingly sensitized to and involved with their newborns. Current childbirth practices are including fathers in the birth process of their infants rather than leaving them in the waiting room with nothing to do but watch a football game on TV. Fathers are often passionate, confused, and puzzled about the wide of range of feelings that emerge at the birth of their infants. However, because of the lack of adequate preparation, fathers, too often, pass on to mothers the overwhelming responsibility of taking care of a newborn (Fine, 1976). Hence, fathers' education cannot stop at childbirth classes.

Discussion and courses could allow fathers to become acquainted with recent research on fathers' abilities to nurture and caregive and on the importance of fathers in infants' development. Fathers would be also taught that fatherhood is a highly active and interactive process and that fathers' stimulation adds fresh and unique nuances to their infant's socioemotional world. In the midst of cuddling, warmth, and rough-and-tumble play with their father, infants would learn to become more autonomous and social.

Although fathers (primary and secondary caregivers) may not always be overly concerned about the way infants are dressed and the mess they make while eating, fathers can neither be considered second rate mothers, mere babysitters, nor mother helpers—far less competent than mothers—nor heroes whenever they have successfully burped their baby or properly changed a diaper. The present study has indicated that primary caregiving fathers are indeed as competent as mothers in caregiving and nurturing their infant. Fathers' confidence and self-efficacy perception would be enhanced by giving new fathers opportunities to practice basic baby-care skills such as holding, comforting, diapering, feeding, and bathing their baby.

Fathers could also be given time to interact alone with their infants and assume total responsibility for their care. The current study indicates that in nontraditional families primary caregiving fathers have multiple opportunities for one-to-one interaction with their infants. In traditional families such opportunities are often missing between infants and their secondary caregiving fathers. Once at home, secondary caregiving fathers usually interact with their infant in the presence of their spouse, that is, in a triadic situation. This situation may limit the ways they relate to their infant and achieve a closer relationship. Therefore, based on the behavior of primary caregiving fathers when alone with their infant, and the invaluable experience they offer to their infant in play, exploration and autonomy, it is suggested that all fathers could be given opportunities to be alone with their infant and to assume the sole responsibility of their care. It is only when they become fully involved and responsible for their infant's care that fathers will be able to experience the full range of meanings encapsulated in fatherhood.

Literature abounds in terms differentiating between male and female characteristics. Males have been described as aggressive, rational, instrumental, competitive, outward looking, and unable to sustain emotional closeness. Females have been characterized as, gentle, supportive, receptive, and expressive, but lacking of ambition. This study has shown that primary caregiving fathers were sensitive, affectionate, and supportive, not because they were more feminine or less masculine than traditional fathers, but because they were capable of experiencing and expressing a wide array human feelings. The example these fathers and their spouse provide to their children could eliminate or at least narrow down gender differences in upbringing.

This study suggests that egalitarian child rearing does not begin by giving dolls to boys and trucks to girls, but from modeling. Fathers and mothers who share equally the outside work and child-care obligations provide a model of egalitarian parenting. They show that parents, whatever their gender, could be nurturant, emotional, and caring, as well as independent, rational, and instrumental. These parents no longer feel compelled to mold a masculine outlook in their sons and a feminine one in their daughters. Their live example encouraged their children to form expectations and life choices that go beyond gender. The convergence and rapprochement of women's and men's roles thus allow children from nontraditional families to expand their horizons and to develop free from the constraints imposed by gender-role stereotypes.

The affiliative and attachment behaviors of primary caregiving fathers in two-parent families have indicated that fathers are as capable as mothers in caregiving, in giving and receiving affection, and in being attuned to their infants. Under stressful and nonstressful conditions, infants were found to be more attached to their father than to their mother when their father assumed primary caregiving duties. These findings have far-reaching implications regarding child-custody resolution in divorce disputes, because it may no longer be assumed that mothers are necessarily the most capable and appropriate custodial parents.

In our technological world women are becoming as qualified and as capable as men to pursue prestigious careers. Yet, men's involvement in child care is limited and will continue to be limited as long as work and family policies do not restructure the world of work. In the current study, primary caregiving fathers usually enjoyed flexible hours and could schedule their working hours allowing time for child care. By contrast, secondary caregiving fathers and mothers often felt that they did not have any leeway in changing their working hours. Finally, primary caregiving mothers felt they had to abandon their careers in order to take care of their infant.

In comparison to European countries such as France, Finland, Sweden, Germany, and Austria, the United States shows a vacuum in family-policies legislation. For the first time, in 1993, the Family and Medical Leave Act (Kamerman & Kahn, 1991) was passed by Congress. It requires employers of fifty or more people to provide all eligible employees twelve weeks of unpaid job-guaranteed leave with health benefits. Yet no income protection was mentioned. As of now only five states (California, Hawaii, New Jersey, New York, and Rhode Island) have required employers to provide mothers with partial paid leave under the Temporary Disability Legislation (TDL) that extends to the limited period of up to six months (Kamerman & Kahn, 1991).

A closer look at Swedish extensive parental leave and work policies that were geared toward greater gender equality may enlighten the direction of social reforms in the United States. Under the government of Olah Palmer, Sweden in 1974 promulgated seven–month paid leave of absence that could be shared between spouses after the birth of their infant (Jackson, 1983). Subsequently, this law was revised to expand parental job-protected leave to up to fifteen months (Kamerman & Kahn, 1991). Also, fifteen-month parental leave of absence may be taken on a full- or part-time basis during the eight years following the child's birth and may be used in as little as two–hour units at a time. These flexible work policies have given parents the opportunity to reduce their working hours from eight to six hours and to choose part-time employment in order to take care of their young children at home. As a result, Swedish fathers with infants spend more time in child care and house-related activities than do fathers in others countries, while Swedish mothers with infants spend more time in paid work and less time in domestic work. Another consequence of these generous parental policies is the decline in the number of infants attending Sweden's extensive public infant day-care facilities. In 1987, only 2 percent of infants less than one year of age attended such facilities (Sundstrom, 1991).

Extrapolating from this example, one may promulgate U.S. parental and work policies that allow for a paid leave of absence after the baby's birth that could be used in two-hour to half-day units by parents. Parents could thus be given the opportunity to reduce the number of their work hours in order to alternate outside employment and child care during the the first years of their infant's life. Flexible work schedule and job sharing added to part-time employment possibilities would create a more satisfying balance between work and family life. These new policies would allow traditional fathers to spend more time in child care and traditional mothers to resolve their dilemma of abandoning a challenging career to take care of their children or feeling guilty of abandoning their children to pursue a career. They would also provide a solution to the often dreaded alternative of leaving very young infants in day-care facilities and wondering about the potential risks of such care on socioemotional development.

Parents have become increasingly aware of detrimental effects of extensive day care for infants less than one-year old. Early infant day care may affect the security of attachment by reducing infants' confidence in the availability and responsiveness of care and their sense of effectiveness in eliciting such a care (Sroufe, 1988). Infants in day care may also feel unwanted and unwantable (Bowlby, 1965). In the words of Sroufe (1988),

> Secure attachment is not something inherent in the infant; it is a product of the infant caregiver interactive history. Infants who by the end of the first year are securely attached have experienced consistently responsive care. They have been picked up when seeking contact, comforted when distressed, and engaged with sensitively. Their gestures have been imbued with meaning, and they have been empowered by a responsive social environment. The securely attached infant has come to expect such emotional availability and responsiveness from the social world. (p. 285)

Disturbance of the mother-infant relationship may also interfere with the tasks of limit setting and self-control in toddlerhood. Belsky's (1988) findings indicate that infants less than one year old experiencing twenty or more hours a week of nonmaternal care were at greater risk of developing insecure-avoidant attachment and consequent socioemotional personality disturbance. Preschool and school-age children who had experienced as infants full-time day care have been found to be more aggressive and hyperactive, to have poor peer relationships and poor work habits, and to be more difficult to discipline than children of the same age who had not experienced full-time day care as infants (Barton & Schwarz, 1981; Belsky, 1988; Schwarz, Strickland & Krolick, 1974).

Having one of the parents at home actively involved in the care of their infant would facilitate the development of secure attachment and thereby allow infants to form a set of expectations about the social world and about themselves as worthy of care. Such child-care arrangement would ensure better conditions for optimum socioemotional development.

The importance of secure attachment as a means of social control in preventing delinquency cannot be glossed over. Time and time again social control theorists (Glueck & Glueck, 1950; Hirschi, 1969; Kornhauser, 1978) have explained that parental love, affection, and respect provide the bridge to the belief in the social norms. Children who are not attached to their parents have no stakes in conformity. They feel free to break the rules and to deviate. With the disappearance of the extended family, the breakdown of the nuclear family, and mothers joining the work force, society witnesses an increase in the number of latch-key children,[2] youth in need of supervision,[3] and infants in full-time day care. Paradoxically, the breakdown and changes in the traditional family structure have had the beneficial effect of unleashing fathers' undiscovered potential as competent and nurturant caregivers. Parental leave, job protection, part-time employment, and flexible work schedule would allow fathers in families fortunate enough to manage without two incomes to invest in their infant's development. They would thereby avoid the detrimental effects of extensive day care and provide a practical solution to the phenomenon of anomic children by preventing it from its inception.

Primary caregiving fathers emerge in this study as competent caregivers, exciting play partners, and nurturant and affectionate companions who stimulate their infant's sociability and autonomous behavior. These new competencies ought to be recognized and strengthened in all fathers—traditional or not—in order to maximize fathers' beneficial influence in early childhood and to create a new stabilizing force in the weakening nuclear family.

NOTES

1. *Statistical Abstract of the United States 1994*, No. 114, p. 386. Fathers caring for their infant in their home constituted 21.6%; nonrelative caring for infant in another home, 20.5%; grandparent caring for infant in another home, 14.3%; organized child care facilities, 11.5%; day/group care center 9.8%; grandparent caring for infant in infant's home, 8.7%; mother caring for infant at work, 7.6%; nonrelative caring for infant in infant's home, 7.5%; other relative caring for infant in another home, 5.6%; other relative caring for infant in infant's home, 2.7%; and nursery school/preschool 1.7%.

2. Siegel & Senna, 1994; Weisberg, 1988; Whisler, 1991.

3. Arthur & Erickson, 1992; Dorrell, 1992; Heflin & Rudy, 1991; Levitan & Schillmoeller, 1991; Moses & Kopplin, 1992; Powers, Eckenrode, & Jaklitsch, 1990; Rafferty & Shinn, 1991; Schorr, 1988; Whitbeck & Simons, 1990.

Appendix A: Parents' Interview Guide

1. Did you feel camera conscious when you were videotaped?

2. If yes, could you mention some of changes that have occurred in your behavior?

3. What is your age range? Age: 20–25, 26–30, 31–40, 40+.

4. Education: Did you finish high school?

5. Did you study in college?

6. Do you have a college degree? If yes, in what?

7. Do you work full-time outside of your home?

8. If not, how many days a week do you work?

9. What about your spouse?

10. Could you describe your schedule?

11. Did you nurse your baby?

12. If yes, for how long?

13. Who takes care of the baby when you are at work?

14. How many days a week do you take care of your baby?

15. How many days a week does your spouse take care of the baby?

16. When you come back from work, does your spouse stay or leave?

17. When you are both at home, who changes the diapers?

18. When you are both at home, who feeds the baby?

19. When you are both at home, who gives the baby a bath?

20. When you are both at home, who comforts the baby?

21. When you are both at home, who puts the baby to sleep?

22. When the baby cries, to whom does he or she generally go for comfort or to be picked up?

23. When the baby is scared or under stress, what does he or she usually do?

24. When the baby is sick, who gets up at night?

25. When the baby is not sick but wakes up at night, who takes care of him or her?

26. Could you tell me everything you did yesterday with your infant?

27. Could you tell me everything your spouse did yesterday with your infant?

28. Could you tell me everything you did last weekend with your infant?

29. Could you tell me everything your spouse did last weekend with your infant?

30. What sort of things do you do together as a family on weekdays?

31. What sort of things do you do together on weekends?

32. In general, how does you child react to strangers?

33. Does your baby cry a lot? Under what circumstances does he or she usually cry?

34. How many children do you have?

35. How old are they?

36. [For children under school age] Where do they spend their day?

37. Do you have a babysitter?

38. If yes, how many hours does she or he babysit?

39. When both of you are at home, who takes care of the baby?

40. Do you often play with the baby? What type of play?

41. Do you believe that your way of life has changed since the birth of your baby?

42. If yes, could you mention some of those changes?

43. For how long have you had this child-care arrangement?

44. What type of child-care arrangement did you have before?

45. Would you prefer some other kind of arrangement? If yes, which one?

46. In your opinion, how should caregiving duties be shared between husband and wife?

47. Would you like to be employed outside the home?

48. If yes, how many days or hours a week?

49. [For families in which fathers are primary caregivers] It is a new trend for many U.S. fathers to take care of their infants while mothers are at work. Could you tell me how you came up with this type of arrangement?

50. Did you consider some alternative child-care arrangement for you child?

51. Have you ever considered using day care for your infant? Why yes? Why no?

Appendix B: Behavioral Definitions of Parents' and Infants' Behaviors

The dependent measures for the affiliative and attachment behaviors of parents and infants received the following behavioral definitions.

The first dependent measure, *Parent's Affiliative Behavior*, was analyzed into: holds, looks, talks to child, plays with books, plays games, plays rough-and-tumble.

1. *Holds* was coded once for each twenty-second period in which the parent supported the baby's body or weight for purposes other than rough-and-tumble play. Examples included the baby sitting on the parent's lap or the parent picking up the baby.

2. *Looks* was coded once for each twenty-second period in which the parent gazed at the baby. There had to be a deliberate intent to look at the baby. If the baby was not in the parent's field of vision, such as when the baby was riding on the parent's back or when the parent was reading to the child sitting on his or her lap facing the book, then there had to be bending toward the child or bodily movement to indicate the parent's deliberate intent to look.

3. *Talks to child* was coded once for each twenty-second period in which the parent vocalized to the child. Vocalization could include a single word, whole sentence, motherese, or adult-type talk. Singing was not counted as an instance of talking.

4. *Play Interaction*
    a. *Plays with books* was coded once for each twenty-second period in which the parent "read" any version of books. Photographs or other forms of illustration that were not in book form were not counted as instances of playing with books.

b. *Plays games* was coded once for each twenty-second period in which the parent engaged in games such as Peek-a-boo, Pat-a-cake, finger plays, or sang songs or said rhymes.

c. *Plays rough-and-tumble* was coded once for each twenty-second period in which the parent played very physically with the goal of vigorously stimulating the child by the enjoyment of bodily movement. Examples of such play included holding the baby up in the air, putting the baby upside down, tossing or bouncing baby.

The second dependent measure, *Parent's Attachment Behavior*, was analyzed into caregives and displays affection.

1. *Caregiving* was coded once for each twenty-second period in which the parent gave the baby a bottle, or food, or diapered the baby, or cleaned the baby's face.   Mere soothing was not coded as instance of caregiving.

2. *Displays affection* was coded once for each twenty-second period in which the parent hugged, kissed, or soothed the child. Verbal endearments such as "honey" or "dear" were not coded as display of affection.

The third dependent measure, *Infant's Affiliative Behavior*, was analyzed into the following behaviors: resists parent's activity, initiates an activity, involves parent in activity, plays together, plays alone, looks, laughs, and vocalizes.

1. *Resists parent's activity* was coded once for each twenty-second period in which the child refused to engage in the parent's activity by ignoring what the parent showed, moving away, or continuing his or her own activity despite the parent's repeated attempts to engage the child's attention.

2. *Initiates activity* was coded once for each twenty-second period in which the infant abandoned an activity in order to engage in a new type of activity not already initiated by the parent.

3. *Involves parent* was coded once for each twenty-second period in which the parent abandoned an activity that he or she was engaged in or had just initiated in order to engage in the activity initiated by the child.

4. *Play together* was coded once for each twenty-second period in which both parent and child were engaged in the same activity.

5. *Plays alone* was coded once for each twenty-second period the child

was engaged by himself or herself in an activity and ignored the parent.

6. *Looks* was coded once for each twenty-second period in which the infant's head was turned in the parent's direction and lifted upward.

7. *Laughs or smiles* was coded once for each twenty-second period in which a facial expression occurred in which the brows were not drawn together and the corners of the mouth were retreated and raised, or when a joyful type of vocalization was emitted by the child.

8. *Vocalizes* was coded once for each twenty-second period in which a directed nondistress vocalization occurred. Instances of vocalization were simple baby sounds, babbles, or sentences. Fussing or laughing were not coded as instances of vocalization.

The fourth dependent measure, *Infant's Attachment Behavior*, was analyzed into the following behaviors: displays affection, moves away, explores objects, approaches, in proximity, clings.

1. *Displays affection* was coded once for every twenty-second period in which the child kissed or hugged the parent.

2. *Moves away* was coded once for every twenty-second period in which the child moved away from the parent, and even if the child was followed by the parent afterwards.

3. *Explores object* was coded once for every twenty-second period in which the child looked or touched an object that was not a usual toy, whether in the parent's proximity or not.

4. *In proximity* was coded once for every twenty-second period in which the child's hand could reach the parent's upper body.

5. *Approaches* was coded once for every twenty-second period in which the child moved within a two-foot radius of the parent.

6. *Clings or climbs* was coded once for every twenty-second period in which the child touched the parent's body as a sign of distress.

The fifth dependent measure, *Infant's Affiliative Behavior under Stress*, was analyzed into the following behaviors: joins stranger's activity, ignores stranger's activity, plays alone, smiles or laughs, vocalizes.

1. *Joins stranger's activity* was coded once for each twenty-second period in which the child abandoned the activity he or she was engaged in order to engage in the activity initiated by the stranger.

2. *Ignores stranger* was coded once for each twenty-second period in which the child refused to engage in the stranger's activity by ignoring

what the stranger showed, moving away, or continuing his or her own activity despite the stranger's repeated attempts to engage the child's attention.

3. *Plays alone* was coded once for each twenty-second period in which the child engaged in an activity by himself or herself while ignoring the stranger.

4. *Smiles or laughs* was coded once for each twenty-second period in which the child emitted a happy vocalization.

5. *Vocalizes* was coded once for each twenty-second period in which the child emitted any nondistress vocalization that included any simple baby sound, babble, or sentence.

The sixth dependent measure, *Infant's Attachment Behaviors under Stress*, was analyzed into: in proximity of father or mother, approaching father or mother, looking at father or mother, body turned toward mother or father, resisting father or mother, physical contact with father or mother.

1. *In proximity* of father or mother was coded once for each twenty-second period in which the child's hand could reach the upper body of the adult concerned.

2. *Approaches* father or mother was coded once for each twenty-second period in which the child moved within a two-foot radius of the adult concerned.

3. *Looks* at father or mother was coded once for each twenty-second period in which the child's head was turned in the direction of the adult concerned.

4. *Body turned toward* father or mother was coded once for each twenty-second period in which the child's body was turned toward the adult concerned.

5. *Physically resists* father or mother was coded once for each twenty-second period in which the child physically pushed the adult away or arched his or her back to escape.

6. *Pick up or physical contact* with father or mother was coded once for each twenty-second period in which the child was picked up by the parent concerned. Other instances included the child's physical contact with any part of the parent's body such as knees or legs.

The *Indicators of Stress* were the following: stranger holding the infant, whining, screaming.

1. *Stranger contact with baby* was coded once for each twenty-second

period in which the stranger picked up or touched the baby.

2. *Whines* was coded once for each twenty-second period in which the child expressed mild distress vocalized by whining.

3. *Screams* was coded once for each twenty-second period in which the child expressed intense distress by screaming and crying.

Appendix C: Coding Sheets for Parents' and Infants' Behaviors

C1: Parents' Affiliative and Attachment Behaviors under Nonstressful Conditions									
	1	2	3	.	.	28	29	30	Total
Holds									
Looks at									
Talks to Child									
Plays with Books									
Games Conventional									
Rough and Tumble									
Caregives									
Displays Affection									

C2: Infants' Affiliative and Attachment Behaviors under Nonstressful Conditions									
	1	2	3	.	.	28	29	30	Total
Resists Activity									
Initiates Activity									
Involves Parent									
Plays Together									
Plays Alone									
Looks at Parent									
Smiles or Laughs									
Vocalizes									
Displays Affection									
Moves Away									
Explores Objects									
Approaches									
In Proximity									
Clings or Climbs									

C3: Infants' Affiliative and Attachment Behaviors under Stress									
Stranger Activity	1	2	3	4	.	.	.	15	Total
joins									
resists/ignores									
plays alone									
Smiles or Laughs									
Vocalizes									
In Proximity									
father									
mother									
Approaches									
father									
mother									
Looks at									
father									
mother									
Body Turned toward									
father									
mother									
Physically Resists									
father									
mother									
Physical Contact									
father									
mother									
Stranger Picks up Baby									
Whines									
Screams									

Appendix D: Intersession Reliability of Parents' and Infants' Behaviors

Table D.1
Reliability of Parents' Behaviors: Session I versus Session II

Session 1	Session 2							
	A	B	C	D	E	F	G	H
A Holds	.41**							
B Looks at Child		.027						
C Talks to Child			.54**					
D Plays with Book				.33**				
E Conventional Games					.25*			
F Rough & Tumble						.45**		
G Caregives							.59**	
H Displays Affection								.54**

Note: The above measures were obtained by computing Pearson r correlation. *$p<.05$; **$p<.01$.

Table D.2
Reliability of Infants' Affiliative Behaviors in a Nonstressful Situation:
Session 1 versus Session 2

| | | | | | **Session 2** | | | |
	A	**B**	**C**	**D**	**E**	**F**	**G**	**H**
Session 1								
A Resists Parent	.48**							
B Initiates Activity		.48**						
C Parent Joins			.46**					
D Plays Together				.54**				
E Plays Alone					.47**			
F Looks at Parent						.53**		
G Smiles/Laughs							.55**	
H Vocalizes								.51**

Note: The above measures were obtained by computing Pearson $\underline{r}$ correlation. **$\underline{p}$<.01.

Table D.3
Reliability of Infants' Attachment Behaviors in a Nonstressful Situation:
Session 1 versus Session 2

| | | | | **Session 2** | | |
	A	**B**	**C**	**D**	**E**	**F**
Session 1						
A Displays Affection	.09					
B Moves Away		.39**				
C Explores Object			.41**			
D Approaches				.30*		
E In Proximity					.28*	
F Clings						.59*

Note: The above measures were obtained by computing Pearson $\underline{r}$ correlation.
*$\underline{p}$<.05; **$\underline{p}$<.01.

Table D.4
Reliability of Infants' Behaviors under Stress:
Session 1 versus Session 2

		Session 2						
		A	B	C	D	E	F	G
Session 1								
A	Joins Stranger	.67**						
B	Resists Stranger		.74**					
C	Plays Alone			.48**				
D	Smiles or Laughs				.47**			
E	Vocalizes					.44**		
F	Proximity Father						.54**	
G	Proximity Mother							.68**

		Session 2						
		H	I	J	K	L	M	N
Session 1								
H	Approaches Father	.23						
I	Approaches Mother		.001					
J	Looks at Father			.49**				
K	Looks at Mother				.61**			
L	Turned Toward Father					.63**		
M	Turned Toward Mother						.62**	
N	Resists Father							.39**

Table D.4 cont.
Reliability of Infants' Behaviors under Stress:
Session 1 versus Session 2

	Session 2						
	O	P	Q	R	S	T	U
Session 1							
O Resists Mother	.08						
P Contact with Father		.69**					
Q Contact with Mother			.75**				
R Stranger Picks Up Baby				.15			
S Resists Stranger					.50**		
T Whines						.69**	
U Screams							.53**

Note: The above measures were obtained by computing Pearson r correlation. **$p<.01$.

Appendix E: Parents' Background Information

Table E.1
Academic Degree: Frequency Count

	Prim	Fa	Second	Mo	Second	Fa	Prim	Mo
	n	Pct	n	Pct	n	Pct	n	Pct
BA/BS	3	21%	4	28%	7	50%	9	64%
MA	1	7%	5	36%	1	7%	3	21%
JD	4	29%	1	7%	0	0%	0	0%
PhD	1	7%	1	7%	0	0%	1	7%
PSY/DDS/MD	0	0%	1	7%	4	29%	0	0%
None	3	21%	2	14%	1	7%	1	7%
PhD Student	2	14%	0	0%	1	7%	0	0%
	14	99%*	14	100%	14	100%	14	100%

Notes: Prim Fa = Primary Caregiving Fathers; Sec Fa = Secondary Caregiving Fathers; Prim Mo = Primary Caregiving Mothers; Sec Mo = Secondary Caregiving Mothers.
*Due to rounding error some percentages do not sum to 100%.

Appendix F: Mean Frequencies of Parents' and Infants' Behaviors in a Nonstressful Situation

Table F.1
Mean Frequencies of the Various Caregivers' Behaviors Toward Their Infants in a Nonstressful Situation

Behavior	Prim Fa		Sec Mo		Sec Fa		Prim Mo	
	n = 14		n = 14		n = 14		n = 14	
Affiliative Beh	Mean	SD	Mean	SD	Mean	SD	Mean	SD
Holds	8.18	4.63	7.43	5.34	6.71	4.89	4.43	5.51
Looks at	27.32	2.59	26.92	1.37	27.64	2.19	28.68	.84
Talks to Child	25.07	6.45	22.53	7.12	26.07	10.94	25.61	5.04
Plays w Books	5.00	5.67	2.68	3.64	2.04	2.49	2.07	3.58
Games	2.04	1.82	1.93	1.86	4.57	12.68	2.86	2.24
Rough & Tumble	1.36	1.18	.14	.31	2.11	2.68	.36	.72
Attachment Beh								
Caregives	2.11	2.70	1.18	1.09	.64	.94	1.46	2.58
Displays Affection	2.75	1.89	.57	.65	.79	.96	1.14	.99

Notes: Prim Fa = Primary Caregiving Fathers: Sec Mo = Secondary Caregiving Mothers; Sec Fa = Secondary Caregiving Fathers; Prim Mo = Primary Caregiving Mothers; Beh = Behavior. Parents' behavior coding ranged from 0 to 30 time segments.

Table F.2
Mean Frequencies of Infants' Behaviors Toward Their Various Caregivers in a Nonstressful Situation

	Prim Fa		Sec Mo		Sec Fa		Prim Mo	
Behavior	n = 14		n = 14		n = 14		n = 14	
Affiliative Beh	Mean	SD	Mean	SD	Mean	SD	Mean	SD
Resists Parent	4.18	2.03	5.29	3.03	4.04	2.92	3.29	2.69
Initiates Activity	8.54	3.34	6.68	2.31	5.07	20.8	5.11	2.82
Involves Parent	9.89	4.06	7.04	2.91	5.04	2.19	5.43	2.14
Plays Together	10.75	5.27	8.50	4.84	10.54	6.02	11.36	6.18
Plays Alone	2.07	2.29	3.61	3.63	3.89	3.62	2.75	4.56
Looks at Parent	4.86	3.46	4.18	2.71	4.29	2.89	4.85	2.71
Smiles/Laughs	6.86	4.77	4.93	4.34	7.04	4.14	6.79	3.47
Vocalizes	14.61	4.36	12.18	5.92	14.14	6.77	13.11	7.00
Attachment Beh								
Displays Affection	.36	.50	.00	.00	.04	.13	.29	.51
Moves Away	6.43	2.81	6.32	3.47	4.29	2.35	4.29	2.87
Explores Objects	6.68	3.07	6.42	3.14	4.82	2.42	5.32	2.62
Approaches	4.82	2.43	3.92	2.17	3.64	2.10	4.10	2.90
In Proximity	12.61	6.99	11.86	6.00	13.96	5.61	12.07	7.33
Clings	.14	.31	.18	.42	.75	1.48	1.14	2.31

Notes: Infants' behavior coding ranged from 0 to 30 time segments.
Prim Fa = Primary Caregiving Fathers; Sec Mo = Secondary Caregiving Mothers;
Sec Fa = Secondary Caregiving Fathers; Prim Mo = Primary Caregiving Mothers.
Beh = Behavior.

Bibliography

Abelin, E. L. (1971).   The role of the father in the separation-individuation process. In J. B. McDevitt & C. F. Settlage (eds.), *Separation-individuation* (pp. 229–252). New York: International Universities Press.

_____. (1975).   Some further observations and comments on the earliest role of the father. *International Journal of Psychoanalysis, 56,* 293–302.

_____. (1980).   Triangulation, the role of the father and the origins of core gender identity during the rapprochement subphase. In R. Lax, S. Bach & A. Burland (eds.),   *Rapprochement: The critical subphase of separation-individuation* (pp. 151–169). New York: Jason Aronson.

Ainsworth, M. D. S. (1962).   The effects of maternal deprivation: A review of findings and controversy in the context of research strategy.   In *Deprivation of maternal care: A reassessment of its effects* (pp. 97–165). Geneva: World Health Organization.

_____. (1963).   The development of infant-mother interaction among the Ghanda. In B. M. Foss (ed.), *Determinants of infant behavior (Vol. 2).* London: Methuen.

_____. (1964).   Patterns of attachment behavior shown by the infant in interaction with his mother. *Merrill-Palmer Quarterly, 10,* 51–58.

_____. (1967).   *Infancy in Uganda: Infant care and the growth of love.* Baltimore: Johns Hopkins Press.

_____. (1973). The development of infant-mother attachment. In B. Caldwell & H. Ricciuti (eds.), *Review of child development research (Vol. 3)* (pp. 1–94). Chicago: University of Chicago Press.

Ainsworth, M. D. S., Bell, S. M., & Stayton, D. J. (1974).   Infant-mother attachment and social development: Socialisation as a product of reciprocal responsiveness to signals. In M. P. M. Richards (ed.),   *The integration of a child into a social world* (pp. 99–135). Cambridge, England: Cambridge University Press.

Ainsworth, M. D. S., Blehar, M. C., Waters E., & Wall, S. N. (1978). *Patterns of attachment*. Hillsdale, NJ: Erlbaum.

Ainsworth, M. D. S., & Wittig, B. A. (1969). Attachment and exploratory behavior of one-year-olds in a Strange Situation. In B. M. Foss (ed.), *Determinants of infant behavior (Vol. 4)* (pp. 111–136). London: Methuen.

Applegate, J. S. (1987). Beyond the dyad: Including the father in separation-individuation. *Child and Adolescent Social Work*, 4(2), 92–105.

Arthur, R., & Erickson, E. (1992). *Gangs and schools*. Holmes Beach, FL: Learning Publications. (ERIC Document Reproduction Service No. ED 358204).

Bailey, W. T. (1982). Affinity: An ethological theory of the infant-father relationship. Paper presented at the 3rd International Conference on Infant Studies, Austin, TX.

Ban, P. L., & Lewis, M. (1974). Mothers and fathers, girls and boys: Attachment behavior in the one year old. *Merrill-Palmer Quarterly*, 20, 195–204.

Barton, M., & Schwarz, J. (1981, August). Day care in the middle class: Effects in elementary school. Paper presented at the American Psychological Association's Annual Convention, Los Angeles.

Bell, S. M. (1970). The development of the concept of the object as related to infant-mother attachment. *Child Development*, 41, 291–311.

Belsky, J. (1979). Mother-father-infant interactions: A naturalistic observational study. *Developmental Psychology*, 15, 601–607.

_____. (1980). A family analysis of parental influence on infant exploratory competence. In F. A. Pedersen (ed.), *The father-infant relationship: Observational studies in the family setting* (pp. 87–110). New York: Praeger.

_____. (1986). Infant day care: A cause for concern? *Zero to Three*, 6(6), 1–7.

_____. (1988). The "effects" of infant day care reconsidered. *Early Childhood Research Quarterly*, 3, 235–272.

Bowlby, J. (1965). *Child care and the growth of love*. Baltimore: Penguin.

_____. (1969). *Attachment and loss: Attachment (Vol. 1)*. New York: Basic Books.

_____. (1973). *Attachment and loss: Separation (Vol. 2)*. New York: Basic Books.

_____. (1980). *Attachment and loss: Sadness and depression (Vol. 3)*. New York: Basic Books.

Bretherton, I. (1985). Attachment theory: Retrospect and prospect. In I. Bretherton & E. Waters (eds.), *Growing points of attachment: Theory and research* (pp. 3–35). Monographs of the Society for Research in Child Development, 50(1–2, Serial No. 209).

Bridges, L. J., Connell, J. P., & Belsky, J. (1988). Similarities and differences in infant-mother and infant-father interaction in the Strange Situation: A component process analysis. *American Psychological Association, 24*(1), 92–100.

Bronfenbrenner, U. (1977). Toward an experimental ecology of human development. *American Psychologist, 32,* 513–531.

Clarke-Stewart, K. A. (1978). And daddy makes three: The father's impact on mother and young child. *Child Development, 49,* 466–478.

———. (1980). The father's contribution to children's cognitive and social development in early childhood. In F. A. Pedersen (ed.), *The father-infant relationship: Observational studies in a family setting* (pp. 111–146). New York: Praeger.

Cohen, L. J., & Campos, J. J. (1974). Father, mother, and stranger as elicitors of attachment behaviors in infancy. *Developmental Psychology, 10,* 146–154.

Connolly, K., & Smith P. K. (1972). Reactions of preschool children to a strange observer. In N. B. Jones (ed.), *Ethological Studies of Child Behavior* (pp. 157–172). Cambridge, England: Cambridge University Press.

Defrain, J. (1979). Androgynous parents who tell who they are and what they need. *Family Co-ordinator, 28,* 237–243.

Dickstein, S., & Parke, R. D. (1988). Social referencing in infancy: A glance at fathers and marriage. *Child Development, 59,* 506–511.

Dollard, J., & Miller, N. E. (1950). *Personality and psychotherapy.* New York: McGraw-Hill.

Dorrell, L. D. (1992). Just take your time and keep it between the lines: Rural education and the at-risk student. Paper presented at the Annual Convention of the National Rural Education Association, Traverse City, MI. (ERIC Document Reproduction Service No. ED 355073).

Emde, R. N. (1981). Changing models of infancy and the nature of early development: Remodeling the foundation. *Journal of the American Psychoanalytic Association, 29,* 179–219.

Ericksen, J. A., Yancey, W. L., & Ericksen, E. P. (1979, May). The division of family roles. *Journal of Marriage and the Family,* 301–313.

Erikson, E. H. (1950). *Childhood and Society.* New York: Norton.

Feldman S., & Ingham, M. (1975). Attachment behavior: A validation study in two age groups. *Child Development, 46,* 319–330.

Field, T. (1978). Interaction behaviors of primary versus secondary caretaker fathers. *Developmental Psychology, 14*(2), 183–184.

Fine, R. A. (1976). Men's entrance to parenthood. *Family Coordinator, 25,* 341–348.

Forrest, T. (1967). The paternal roots of male character development. *Psychoanalytic Review, 54*(2), 277–295.

Freud, S. (1948). *An outline of psychoanalysis.* New York: Norton.

_____. (1955).   Analysis of a phobia in a five-year-old boy. *Standard Edition,*
    (Vol. 10). London: Hogarth. (Original work published 1909).

Frodi, A. M., Lamb, M. E., Hwang, C. P., & Frodi, M. E. (1983).   Father-mother
    infant interaction in traditional and nontraditional Swedish families: A
    longitudinal study. *Alternative Lifestyles,* 5(3), 142–163.

Gleason, J. B. (1975).   Fathers and other strangers: Men's speech to young
    children. In D. P. Dato (ed.), *Language and linguistics.* Washington,
    D.C.: Georgetown University Press.

Glueck, S., & Glueck, E.   (1950).   *Unraveling juvenile delinquency.* Cambridge,
    MA: Harvard University Press.

Golinkoff, R. M., & Ames, G. J. (1977, March).   Do fathers use "motherese"?
    Paper presented at the meeting of the Society for Research in Child
    Development, New Orleans.

Goodwin, W. L., & Driscoll, L. A. (1980).   *Handbook for measurement and
    evaluation in early childhood education.* San Francisco: Jossey-Bass.

Greenberg, M., & Morris, N. (1974).   Engrossment: The newborn's impact upon
    the father. *American Journal of Orthopsychiatry,* 44, 520–531.

Gronseth E. (1975).   Work-sharing families: Adaptations of pioneering families
    with husband and wife in part-time employment. *Acta Sociologica, 18,*
    202–221.

Grossman, K., & Grossman, K. (1980).   The development of relationship patterns
    during the first two years of life. Paper presented to the International
    Congress of Psychology, Leipzig.

Harlow, H. F. (1961). The development of affectional patterns in infant monkeys.
    In B. M. Foss (ed.), *Determinants of infant behaviour, (Vol. I)* (pp.
    75–88). London: Methuen.

Harlow, H. F., & Zimmerman, R. R. (1959).   Affectional responses in the infant
    monkey. *Science, 130,* 421.

Heflin, L. J., & Rudy, K.   (1991).   *Homeless and in need of special education:
    Exceptional children at risk.*   Reston, VA: Council for Exceptional
    Children. (ERIC Document Reproduction Service No. ED 339167).

Henderson, J. (1982).   The role of the father in separation-individuation. *Bulletin
    of the Menninger Clinic,* 46(3), 231–254.

Hirschi, T.   (1969).   *Causes of delinquency.*   Berkeley, CA: University of
    California Press.

Hirshberg, L. M. (1990).   When infants look to their parents: II. Twelve-month-
    olds' response to conflicting parental emotional signals. *Child
    Development,* 61, 1187–1191.

Hirshberg, L. M., & Svejda, M. (1990).   When infants look to their parents:
    I. Infants' social referencing of mothers compared to fathers. *Child
    Development,* 61, 1175–1186.

Hood, J., & Golden, S. (1979). Beating time/making time: The impact of work
    scheduling on mens' family roles. *Family Co-ordinator,* 28, 575–582.

Hull, C. L. (1943). *Principles of human behavior*. New York: Appleton-Century-Crofts.

Jackson, B. (1983). *Fatherhood*. London: George Allen & Unwin.

Kamerman, S. B., & Kahn, A. J. (eds.) (1991). *Child care, parental leave, and the under 3s: Policy innovation in Europe*. New York: Auburn House.

Kauffman, A. L. (1977, April). Mothers' and fathers' verbal interactions with children learning language. Paper presented to the Eastern Psychological Association, Boston.

Keller, H. R., Montgomery, B., Moss, J., Sharp, J., & Wheeler, J. (1975, April). Differential parental effects among one-year-old infants in a stranger and separation situation. Paper presented at the meetings of the Society for Research in Child Development, Denver.

Kornhauser, R. R. (1978). *Social sources of delinquency: An appraisal of analytic models*. Chicago: University of Chicago Press.

Kotelchuck, M. (1976). The infant's relationship to the father: Experimental evidence. In M. E. Lamb (ed.). *The role of the father in child development* (pp. 329–344). New York: Wiley.

Kotelchuck, M., Zelaro, P., Kagan, J., & Spelke, E. (1975). Infant reaction to parental separation when left with familiar and unfamiliar adults. *Journal of Genetic Psychology, 126*, 255–262.

Lamb, M. E. (1976a). Twelve-month-olds and their parents: Interaction in a laboratory playroom. *Developmental Psychology, 12*, 237–244.

_____. (1976b). Interactions between eight month-old children and their fathers and mothers. In M. E. Lamb (ed.), *The role of the father in child development* (pp. 307–327). New York: Wiley.

_____. (1976c). Parent-infant interaction in eight-month-olds. *Child Psychiatry and Human Development, 7*, 56–63.

_____. (1976d). The role of the father: An overview. In M. E. Lamb (ed.), *The role of the father in child development* (pp. 1–63). New York: Wiley.

_____. (1977). Father-infant and mother-infant interaction in the first year of life. *Child Development, 48*, 167–181.

_____. (1978a). Infant social cognition and "second order" effects. *Infant Behavior and Development, 1*, 1–10.

_____. (1978b). Social interaction in infancy and the development of personality. In M. E. Lamb (ed.), *Social and personality development* (pp. 26–49). New York: Holt, Rinehart, & Winston.

_____. (1978c). Qualitative aspects of mother- and father-infant attachments. *Infant Behavior and Development, 1*, 265–275.

_____. (1979). Separation and reunion behaviors as criteria of attachment to mothers and fathers. *Early Human Development, 3/4*, 329–339.

_____. (1980). The development of parent-infant attachments in the first two years of life. In F. A. Pedersen (ed.), *The father-infant relationship: Observational studies in the family setting*. New York: Praeger.

Lamb, M. E. (ed.) (1976). *The role of the father in child development*. New York: Wiley.

_____. (1981). *The role of the father in child development* (2nd ed.). New York: Wiley.

Lamb, M. E., & Goldberg, W. A. (1982). The father-child relationship: A synthesis of biological, evolutionary, and social perspectives. In L. W. Hoffman, R. Gandelman & H. R. Schiffman (eds.), *Parenting: Its causes and consequences* (pp. 55–73). Hillsdale, NJ: Erlbaum.

Lamb, M. E., & Levine, J. A. (1983). The Swedish parental insurance policy: An experiment in social engineering. In M. E. Lamb, & A. Sagi (eds.), *Fatherhood and family policy*, (pp. 39–51). Hillsdale, NJ: Erlbaum.

Leonard, M. (1966). Fathers and daughters. *International Journal of Psychoanalysis*, *47*, 325–334.

Levitan, S. A., & Schillmoeller, S. (1991). *The paradox of homelessness in America*. Washington, DC: George Washington University, Center for Social Policy Studies. (ERIC Document Reproduction Service No. ED 328759).

Lewis, M., Feiring, C., & Weinraub, M. (1981). The father as a member of the child's social network. In M. E. Lamb (ed.), *The role of the father in child development* (pp. 259–294). New York: Wiley.

Lytton, H. (1976). The socialization of two-year-old boys: Ecological findings. *Journal of Child Psychology and Psychiatry*, *17*, 287–304.

MacDonald, K., & Parke, R. E. (1984). Bridging the gap: Parent-child play interaction and peer interactive competence. *Child Development*, *55*, 1265–1277.

Machtlinger, V. J. (1981). The father in psychoanalytic theory. In M. E. Lamb (ed.), *The role of the father in child development* (pp. 113–154). New York: Wiley.

Mahler, M. S., Pine, F., & Bergman A. (1975). *The psychological birth of the human infant: Symbiosis and individuation*. New York: Basic.

Main, M., & Weston, D. R. (1981). The quality of the toddler's relationship to mother and to father, related to conflict behavior and the readiness to establish new relationships. *Child Development*, *52*, 932–940.

Moses, C. E., & Kopplin, D. (1992). Applying humanistic principles to the treatment of runaway and throwaway adolescents. Paper presented at the Annual Convention of the Southwestern Psychological Association, Austin Texas. (ERIC Document Reproduction No. ED 345171).

Newland, K. (1980, May). *Women, men and the division of labor*. Washington, D.C.: Worldwatch Institute.

Ninio, A., & Rinott, N. (1988). Fathers' involvement in the care of their infants and their attributions of cognitive competence to infants. *Child Development*, *59*(3), 652–663.

Parke, R. D., & O'Leary, S. E. (1976). Family interaction in the newborn period:

Some findings, some observations, and some unresolved issues. In K. F. Riegel & J. Meacham (eds.), *The developing individual in a changing world (Vol. II)* (pp. 653–664. *Social and environmental issues.* The Hague: Mouton.

Parke, R. D., & Sawin, B. (1975, April). Infant characteristics and behavior as elicitors of maternal and paternal responsivity in the newborn period. Paper presented at symposium of Society for Research in Child Development, Denver.

Parke, R. D., & Sawin, D. B. (1976). The father's role in infancy: A reevaluation. *The Family Coordinator, 25,* 365–371.

———. (1980). The family in early infancy: Social interactional and attitudinal analyses. In F. A. Pedersen (ed.). *The father-infant relationship in a family setting* (pp. 44–70). New York: Praeger.

Parke, R. D., & Tinsley, B. (1981). The father's role in infancy: Determinants of involvement in caregiving and play. In M. E. Lamb (ed.), *The role of the father in child development* (pp. 429–458). New York: Wiley.

Parsons, T., & Bales, R. F. (1955). *Family socialization and interaction process.* Glencoe, Ill: Free Press.

Pedersen, F. A. (ed.). (1980). *The father-infant relationship: Observational studies in the family setting.* New York: Praeger.

Pedersen, F. A., & Robson, K. S. (1969). Father participation in infancy. *American Journal of Orthopsychiatry, 39,* 466–472.

Pedersen, F. A., Yarrow, L., Anderson, B., & Cain, R. (1979). Conceptualization of father influences in the infancy period. In M. W. Lewis & L. Rosenblum (eds.), *The social network of the developing infant.* New York: Plenum.

Piaget, J. (1954). *The construction of reality in the child.* New York: Basic.

Pleck J., & Rustad, M. (1980). Husbands' and wives' time in family work and paid work in the 1975 and 1976 study of time use. Unpublished manuscript.

Powers, J. L., Eckenrode, J., & Jaklitsch, B. (1990). Maltreatment among runaway and homeless youth. *Child Abuse and Neglect, 14*(1), 87–98.

Radin, N. (1980, July). Childrearing fathers in intact families: An exploration of some antecedents and consequences. Paper presented to a study group on "The role of the father in child development, social policy and the law." Haifa, Israel.

Rafferty, Y., & Shinn, M. (1991). The impact of homelessness on children. *American Psychologist, 46*(11), 1170–1179.

Rebelsky, F., & Hanks, C. (1971). Fathers' verbal interaction with infants in the first three months of life. *Child Development, 42,* 63–68.

Robinson, J. (1977). *Changes in Americans' use of time, 1965 and 1975.* Cleveland: Communications Research Centre, Cleveland State University.

Russel, G. (1983). *The changing role of fathers.* Milton Keynes, Australia: Open

University Press.

Russel, G., & Radojevic, M. (1992). The changing role of fathers? Current understandings and future directions for research and practice. *Infant Mental Health Journal, 13*(4), pp. 296-311.

Sattler, J. M. (1992). *Assessment of children* (3rd ed.). San Diego: Jermone M. Sattler Publisher.

Schaffer, H. R., & Emerson, P. E. (1964). The development of social attachments in infancy. *Monographs of the Society for Research in Child Development, 29*(Serial number 94).

Schorr, L. B. (1988). *Within our reach: Breaking the cycle of disadvantage.* New York: Doubleday.

Schwarz, J. C., Strickland, R. G., & Krolick, G. (1974). Infant day care: Behavioral effects at preschool age. *Developmental Psychology, 10*, 502–506.

Siegel, L. J., & Senna, J. J. (1994). *Juvenile delinquency: Theory, practice and law.* St. Paul, MN: West Pub. Co.

Spelke, E., Zelaro, P., Kagan, J., & Kotelchuck, M. (1973). Father interaction and separation protest. *Developmental Psychology, 9*(1), 83–90.

Sroufe, L. A. (1988). A developmental perspective on day care. *Early Childhood Research Quarterly, 3*, 283–291.

Statistical abstract of the United States 1994, No. 114. Washington, D.C.: U. S. Dept. of Commerce, Bureau of the Census.

Stevenson, M. B., & Lamb, M. E. (1979). Effects of infant sociability and the caretaking environment on infant cognitive performance. *Child Development, 50*, 340–349.

Sundstrom, M. (1991). Sweden: Supporting work, family, and gender equality. In S. B. Kamerman & A. J. Kahn (eds.), *Child care, parental leave, and the under 3s: Policy innovation in Europe* (pp. 171–199). New York: Auburn House.

Weinraub, M., & Frankel, J. (1977). Sex differences in parent-infant interaction during free play, departure and separation. *Child Development, 48*, 1240–1249.

Weisberg, P. G. (1988). Symposium: Social implications and alternatives for families and children in the next decade. Paper presented at the Association for Childhood Education International Convention, Salt Lake City, Utah.

Whisler, J. S. (1991). *The impact of the teacher on students' sense of self: A perspective from a model of mental health.* Aurora, CO: Mid-Continent Regional Educational Lab. (ERIC Document Reproduction Service No. ED 358394).

Whitbeck, L. B., & Simons, R. L. (1990). Life in the streets: The victimization of runaway and homeless adolescents. *Youth and Society, 22*(1), 108–125.

Winnicott, D. W. (1956). Primary maternal preoccupation. In *Collected papers: Through paediatrics to psycho-analysis*, 300–305. London: Tavistock.

Yogman, M. (March, 1977). The goals and structure of face-to-face interaction between infants and fathers. Paper presented at the meetings of the Society for Research in Child Development, New Orleans.

————. (1982). Development of the father-infant relationship. In H. Fitzgerald, B. Lester & M. Yogman (eds.), *Theory and Research in Behavioral Pediatrics*. New York: Plenum.

Yogman, M., Dixon, S., Tronick, E., Adamson, L., Als, H., & Brazelton, T. (1976). Development of infant social interaction with fathers. Paper presented to the Eastern Psychological Association, New York.

Zegiob, L. E., Arnold. S, & Forehand, R. (1975). An examination of observer effects in parent-child interactions. *Child Development*, *46*, 509–512.

Index

About the Author

BRENDA GEIGER is an assistant professor in the Department of Educational Psychology and Statistics at the State University of New York at Albany. Her present areas of scholarly interest include child development, day care, and peer group socialization. Among her earlier publications are *Reform Through Community* and *Family Justice and Delinquency* (both co-authored with Michael Fischer and published by Greenwood Press in 1991 and 1995 respectively).

ISBN 0-313-29919-6

90000>

EAN

9 780313 299193

HARDCOVER BAR CODE